There shall be a tree unto each season to mark the TURNING of the Wheel.

And there shall be a year of MOONS to connect the passage of the seasons.

About this Book

Most witchcraft in America comes from or has been influenced by the witchcraft of the British Isles. *Year of Moons, Season of Trees* explores the Druidic sacred trees native to the British tradition. While most books related to the Druidic trees approach the subject from a scholarly viewpoint, this volume provides history, interpretation, and symbolism in language that is accessible to all.

Year of Moons, Season of Trees is indeed a seed for an enchanted forest of magical and spiritual growth.

About the Author

Pattalee Glass-Koentop was born four days before Hallowe'en, 1943, in Dumas Texas. She has explored astrology, tarot, Qabbala, and other topics. As a Wiccan High Priestess, she has trained covens that continue to practice and teach in California, Arkansas, Louisiana, Virginia, Arizona, Illinois, Colorado, and Missouri, as well as in Texas. Currently living in Texas, she is developing an accredited university extension program in areas related to the Craft. She is also planning the twelfth annual Celebration of Womanhood, to take place in the summer of 1991.

To Write to the Author

We cannot guarantee that every letter written to the author can be answered, but all will be forwarded. Both the author and the publisher appreciate hearing from readers, learning of your enjoyment and benefit from this book. Llewellyn also publishes a bi-monthly news magazine with news and reviews of practical esoteric studies and articles helpful to the student, and some readers' questions and comments to the author may be answered through this magazine's columns if permission to do so is included in the original letter. The author sometimes participates in seminars and workshops, and dates and places are announced in *The Llewellyn New Times*. To write to the author, or to ask a question, write to:

Pattalee Glass-Koentop
c/o *The Llewellyn New Times*
P.O. Box 64383-269, St. Paul, MN 55164-0383, U.S.A.
Please enclose a self-addressed, stamped envelope for reply, or $1.00 to cover costs.

Llewellyn's World Magic Series

Year of Moons, Season of Trees

Mysteries & Rites of Celtic Tree Magic

Pattalee Glass-Koentop

1991
Llewellyn Publications
St. Paul, Minnesota 55164–0383, U.S.A.

Year of Moons, Season of Trees. Copyright ©1991 by Pattalee Glass-Koentop. All rights reserved. Printed in the United States of America. No part of this book may be used or reproduced in any manner whatsoever without written permission from Llewellyn Publications except in the case of brief quotations embodied in critical articles and reviews.

First Edition
First Printing

Cover painting: Robin Wood
Interior illustrations: Robin Wood
Book Design: Terry Buske

Library of Congress Cataloging-in-Publications Data
Glass-Koentop, Pattalee, 1943-
Year of moons, season of trees : mysteries and rites of Celtic tree magic /
Pattalee Glass-Koentop.
p. cm. — (Llewellyn's world magic series)
Includes bibliographical references.
ISBN 0–87542–269–1
1. Magic, Celtic. 2. Trees—Religious aspects. 3. Moon—
Religious aspects. 4. Goddess religion. 5. Ritual. I. Title
II. Series.
BF1622.C45G53   1991
133.4'3'089916—dc20   91–6671
                                                        CIP

Llewellyn Publications
A Division of Llewellyn Worldwide, Ltd.
P.O. Box 64383, St. Paul, MN 55164-0383

This book is dedicated with deepest of love
and the greatest respect
to

Priestess Arianrhod,

who greeted me at the edge of the Circle
and guided me on the pathway.

And to

Priestess Sunna,

who taught me the mysteries of Grainne
and proclaimed me Priestess in my own right.

Other books by the author:

The Silver Lady and Other Poems, 1978
The Magic in Stones, 1989

Forthcoming books:

Prosperity Magic
Cauldron of the Moon
The Time is Rite

CONTENTS

introduction

by Morgan McFarland

When I was a small child, I was always surprised that children whom I had just met knew the same things that I did. We could play hopscotch or jump rope, share and hold conversations with each other's dolls and imaginary friends, and fall into "pretend" roles with very little preparation. Hopscotch designs might vary, jump-rope rhymes might differ by a word or two or three, but, basically, we knew the same things.

I had the same sense of surprise over fifteen years ago upon discovering that people I'd just met shared my religious beliefs. They knew what I knew. Our circles might vary, our ritual runes might differ by a word or a verse; but, basically, we knew the same things. As Children of One Mother, we have done as children do: we share; we trade; and we zealously guard certain secrets. Except there are no secrets in the mysteries of Neo-Paganism.

Some years ago, Pattalee (with whom I had corresponded, met, talked, shared personal and Craft joys and sorrows and rituals for years) began to read about and study my Dianic tradition on her own. Each Moon, she sent me rituals that she had developed along with the bits and pieces that had led her down the Moon's path. I was delighted, and I showed them to members of my Covenstead. Most were as pleased as I; others were quite defensive, as though our "secrets" had been spread about willy-nilly. Of course, Children will be children. Perhaps, in the past decade, we have grown.

Since then, Pattalee has been initiated, queried and quizzed; found to be sound of intuition and lore; and taken through Passage into Dianic High Priestesshood. All of this has taken place after her years as an initiate and as a High Priestess of the Mysteries of her original tradition (which Mysteries, by the Way of the Wicca, she has never revealed to her Dianic teachers).

Why this discourse on secrets and mysteries? It is to tell those of you who are seekers that this is a book from which you can learn much if you are willing to go beyond its printed word to the dedication and truth with which it was written. Also, it is to remind you who are Initiates of what you already know: the mysteries lie within us. Oftimes, a new way to celebrate them refreshes the soul. If the new celebration is so close to the old that it is uncomfortable, then perhaps something has been lost along your way. Remember: there are no secrets in the Mother's Mysteries, but there are always new revelations.

As Her Children, we know the same things. The hopscotch design may differ. The rite is the same. Our growth comes from sharing and accepting.

> Blessed Be.
> Morgan McFarland
> The Covenstead of Morrigana

prologue

It is strange how doing the right thing for the wrong reasons may sometimes turn out for the good in the end! I first began studying the trees because I was surrounded by people whose attitude was: "Oh, well . . . if you don't know about the trees, then you aren't really knowledgeable at all!" Well, the actual comment was more to the effect that under those conditions, I shouldn't even consider myself an initiate, much less a High Priestess!

Unless I was knowledgeable about *their* trees, my years of study and preparation, and the fact that the Elders of my tradition had felt me properly prepared to accept teaching and ritual responsibility for others, did not seem to matter. They may have considered my Elders to be non-initiates, also!

I never had cared for being patronized and became a bit annoyed at the consistent rudeness in that attitude. I set myself a goal at the beginning of one year to research and to write a Moon ritual appropriate to the tree of each Moon. My thought was to learn enough to understand their viewpoint and, perhaps, even intelligently discuss the topic of the Moon trees should it arise around me. Their narrow little horizons, lack of inner vision, and bigoted spiritual myopia provided a challenge which stirred me to mental and emotional action. The result was the expansion of my vistas and horizons which have given me visions filled with splendor and new viewpoints of the God and Goddess. Thank Goddess for certain narrow minds that irritate or stir us to activity! This book is the ultimate result of my response to that challenge many years ago.

To practitioners of any tradition which utilizes the Ogham Tree Calendar in its working: please rest assured that all of the material contained in this volume is solely a result of that research, and the outcome of conversations with others also intrigued by the Sacred Trees and who shared their findings out of that same joy of learning. No Book (or Books) of

Lights and Shadows has been plundered in order to present this. If what I have written strikes a chord or echo of memory, it is because some universal truths are just that — both universal and Truth. They reach our understanding in many forms and are not limited to the knowledge of a select few.

One adjustment I wanted to make was to utilize the scientific style of dating. Rather than using B.C. or A.D. as time designations, as is common in most religious writings, I preferred to use B.C.E. (Before Common Era) and C.E. (Common Era). Somehow, discussing an ancient religious pattern with a dating system which relates to only one of the most recent of all modern religions seemed incongruous and quite out of place. However, using the more common dating method does make for easier understanding for some readers. You may find both forms of dating within this volume. Please just read your familiar system into place when you find its opposite.

The reason for this book is threefold. First, I am impelled to share with others the beauty and depth of connection I found in my studies, and feel I have some small skill in doing so.

Secondly, during the last few years I have met many who are drawn to the God and Goddess, our Lord and Lady, but who live in areas where there are few stores with the needed books and learning materials, and where there are still fewer teachers available with whom to study. The greatest fear I have heard these seekers express is of "doing something wrong." Therefore, this book is a way of "doing things" which they can use, without fear, as the contents have been effectively used for some time.

While there are decided advantages to studying with a group or a qualified teacher, and to being subsequently initiated by such a Circle or teacher, not all of those whom the Goddess has chosen to initiate into Her Service fall into that category. The third reason for this book is to provide seeds of thought for those priests and priestesses who have been called to Her Service, yet who still doubt their right to serve.

Not all seekers find the teachers needed or desired, nor do all receive the formal initiation they seek. All such initiations are in reality (or should be) merely a recognition of that which the Goddess has already done. This is, therefore, a generic Book of Lights and Shadows which can be used by any solitaire or fledgling Circle desiring to worship the Laughing God of Death and Life (the Lord of Light and the Hunt), and the Queen of the Heavens (Mother of All), our Lady Goddess.

To those for whom this book fills a need — use and enjoy. It is oriented to service, to learning, to worship, and to the inner awareness of the Ancient Gods and the individual's relationship with them.

The God and Goddess recognize Their own. I feel it could be hazardous to one's health to refuse to recognize those who have so obviously been chosen for Their service. I would personally prefer not to argue with the Lady regarding what She has done.

This volume will first present an overview of concepts related to lunar calendars and forms of tree worship, then present the Ogham (on which this material is based), which combines both. In the sections following the overview, as "new" concepts or data are presented, you will find yourself remembering it. As you "learn" it, you will pull still more from past, cosmic, or racial memory to flesh out and create what may well have been your practice in lives past.

A brief "generic" ritual, and an explanation of its inner purpose or intent, is included, along with tips on how to create the symbols or ritual aids mentioned in the rite. Next is an overview of ritual practices as presented in this book. The Solar trees represent the Seasons in the Wheel of the Year. Each tree chapter contains some how-to points related to that tree. The Moon Tree rituals section also shares helpful hints for observing each rite. The working portion of the book closes with suggestions for using the rituals and their results and reminders of things to check on and to be sure of before beginning your work.

Supplemental data is provided in the reference section in the back of this volume, including the Ogham, tree information, chants, and more. For those of you who are historians or scholars regarding Celtic topics or the Ogham, please remember that, just as most of you do not agree about which alphabet is which, so the layman has his or her own approach. For myself, I am much more comfortable with the Beth-Luis-Nion (Birch-Rowan-Ash-Alder-Willow) sequencing of the tree season and have used that as the foundation for this work. The various Celtic scholars whom I have consulted were willing to share their views, but because of the generally negative attitudes regarding "alternative religions" within their institutions, preferred to be unidentified. Among their comments were the following responses:

"The B-L-N sequence is historically practical."

"The Beth-Luis-Fearn alphabet is the only accurate system to consider, historically speaking."

"The Ogham, actually, was simply adopted and adapted by the Celts. It is not a form of communication indigenous to that culture."

"There is no historical documentation whatever to authenticate the Beth-Luis-Fearn pattern for the Ogham. The Beth-Luis-Nion sequence is the only one an intelligent person would consider."

"The Beth-Luis-Nion alphabet is a derivation or development for which no one has any real explanation. (Only) the Beth-Luis-Fearn pattern alone has any historical significance."

"I would doubt seriously that it makes any actual difference. There are good reasons for each system and supportive documentation, but (there is) no clear-cut decision point or irrefutable evidence in either direction."

Since even the scholars cannot agree, I will remain with the approach which feels best to me. It is one which has proven itself in ritual practice for several years. Your personal practice, as well, should be based on that which truly feels correct to your inner self, not on that which someone else says is proper or acceptable as far as they are concerned. If you should find that your personal response is stronger with the Birch-Rowan-Alder-Willow-Ash sequence, then create the appropriate rites from your own reading and research so that your system is properly complete.

These rituals have been used in our Training Circle since 1982. When I wrote these rites, I included as much silent symbolism as I could, in the hope that the "excess" would serve as a trigger to aid each of the beginning students to attune, recognize, and develop the inner awareness each already had.

For many, the rituals included in this book may seem overly involved, too wordy, or dramatically ornate. They may be, but consider the purpose for which they were used — to *teach* on deeper levels than can be done with lecture notes.

We all know that true worship and service to the Goddess is done within each of us. It is done without candles, incense, decoration, altar, tools, bell, books, or any other accessories and aids. If it cannot be done in that manner, then it cannot be done at all. We only fool ourselves into thinking we have evolved in spiritual ways.

However, we also know that colors, scents, tonal vibrations, and tokens which are physical-world symbols of those inner truths can be used effectively in harmony with our inner worship. We must remember that the focus for our worship is not the tokens, the aids, or the tools available, but the Lord and Lady.

I am willing as are most teachers to use virtually all means at my disposal to convey meanings or spark learning interests. The choice is yours: you may use these rituals as they are, adapt them to fit your needs, or use them as a springboard to blaze your own trails on the astral plane and in your personal spiritual growth. Whether you are solitary and use these rituals as a meditative focus in your own worship or wish to share them in group working practice, please enjoy your use of this volume. The research which led to its writing and what I learned in the process are very special to me. I am honored to be able to share them with you.

In shared service to the Goddess, God, and the Ancient Ones, Merry Meet, and

Blessed Be,
Pattalee

"...And it once was..."

Ancient Time-Keepers

Imagine living at a time or in an area in which there were no clocks or calendars. A vastly different concept of time would have been required, in contrast to the hectic, hurry-up-and-wait, and keep-track-of-every-second lifestyles we live today. We would have turned to Nature to provide us with the means of measuring our lives, as an examination of various lunar calendars will show.

Most of us assume, all too easily, that everyone else sees everything as we do. Reviewing these various approaches to measuring and recording time makes it evident that differences still exist which must be considered, or for which allowances need to be made.

As we measure time by the world around us, we would first break it into units marked by the light and dark periods that occurred most frequently. However, in their very frequency, one such cycle of light and dark has a habit of merging into the next and into the one after that. We would then use slightly larger units of time as benchmarks in our lives. Differences have existed even in the counting of such simple cycles: Babylonians, Greeks, and early primitive tribes reckoned from dawn to the following sunrise; midnight-to-midnight marked the Egyptian-invented twenty-four hour "days"; Jews and Italians counted from sunset to sunset; and the Teutons determined their time by "nights," not days.

After a few light-and-darks, we would notice changes in the big light in the nighttime sky. Thus the Moon would become our first extended time-keeper and a visible calendar. We would measure time between one full Moon and the next. Women, because their natural menstrual cycles followed the cycles of the Moon, would have been the first keepers of a calendar. In fact, lunar-based calendrical tally sticks have been discovered which may

3

date back to approximately 50,000 B.C.E. Authorities disagree on the actual purpose or use of the tally sticks as well as their age. So the actual dating may fall anywhere between 60,000 and 30,000 B.C.E. Either way, they pre-date the Ogham alphabet we will discuss later as a calendar.

Even without specifics as to which date might be which, we would mark partial Moons by the visible changes in the Moon itself and plan accordingly. We might arrange to meet "when the Moon is at crescent." Or we might plan to complete a particular piece of handiwork or extended chore by the "half Moon," "full Moon," or the "no Moon."

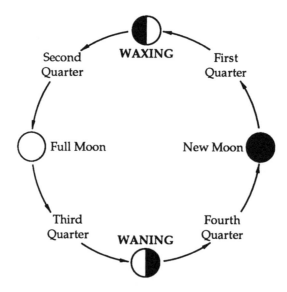

Variations occurred in the manners by which differing cultures marked those longer periods of "days." These ranged from five days in central Asia, six days for the Assyrians, four days in West African tribes, eight days in Rome, and ten days in Egypt. Current seven-day "weeks" are a result of the Babylonian emphasis on the Moon phases and cycles.

In time, we would have realized that the weather altered drastically by the end of three or four Moons. We might have called these changes by their characteristics and eventually come to consider the return of the "Time of Flowers," "Time of Heat," "Time of Harvest," or the "Time of Cold" as a complete cycle of time measurement (what is now referred to as a "season"), regardless of whether we understood the solar patterns involved.

You can see that it would not have taken very long before humankind would have established a means of measuring the passage of time that would greatly resemble what we today call day and night, weeks, months, seasons, and years.

A much more relaxed attitude would have developed regarding activities and plans for daily living. Appointments would be made for general times, such as "sometime tomorrow" or "around midday." Personal relationships would be smoother and less stressful. After all, if you had planned to meet someone "near sunset" and they were fifteen minutes late in arriving, it would make little difference. Who would worry about a quarter of an hour? What are minutes or hours, for that matter?

Significant events to be remembered would be measured by the Moons or seasons which had passed since the event occurred or by other events near it in time. Instead of referring to friends as having married in "such-and-such year," we would recall that their wedding was "six summers ago" or "at the end of the rainy year."

Obviously different cycles are in effect simultaneously. The Sun has a daily impact, a seasonal pattern, and a yearly circuit to consider. The waxing and waning of the Moon follows the path of the Sun, but completes itself roughly every twenty-eight days (almost thirteen times a year), while the Sun circles only once in the year. As we noticed before, the Moon cycle is more evident and visible and thus is more easily measured.

For this reason, almost all early methods of time-keeping calendars were lunar-based. They focused on events of Nature to mark their beginning and end points. In one area the new year might begin with the first Moon after a particular kind of plant or grove of trees leafed out to mark the end of winter. People in another area would consider the first Moon of the year to be the one following the disappearance of the ice on the streams.

The very first calendars were quite simple. They counted days! We can examine records of kings who reigned for thousands of years! If we divide the "years" of their reign by 365.25 — the number of days in a year as we know it — they have amazingly ordinary durations of rulership. In the Larsa List #1 one of the first kings is noted as having reigned for 28,800 years. A series of later kings in Larsa List #2 had combined rulerships which covered 456,000 years. The actual duration of those reigns is 78 years and 1,200 years, respectively.

The example of using the form of calendar with which most of us are more familiar is the longevity of Methusela as mentioned in the Christian Old Testament. When we divide the years of his life by the days in our standard years, we find that he was, indeed, fairly long-lived. But he did not drastically exceed the life-span anyone might expect today.

As late as 2700 to 2500 B.C.E., a different form of time-keeping recorded the "weeks" which had passed. However, this calendar's "week" is not precisely equivalent to the seven-day, Sunday-through-Saturday form we use today. Basically, there were five "working days" in each week with a holiday or three thrown in for rest. Thus the week would generally contain six-and-a-fraction days. With these calendars, the seemingly long reigns become quite normal in length when divided by the roughly six-day week.

These apparent discrepancies appear in both secular and sacred records. One of the reasons for this confusion in religious writings, especially in those of the Christian sect, is that the word for "year" used in the Old Testament has five distinct translations. We find all five "definitions" in use in some passages, depending upon which meaning was used in that particular version of the scriptures. The influence of the language and mores of that particular time and era frequently twisted the resultant interpretations. This practice makes time-keeping definitely a religious art rather than a science when studying Christian writings.

As human beings moved further through time, more practical calendars evolved. The earliest reliable forms were lunar. The Mohammedan calendar, still in use today, is Moon-based. The most commonly used calendar is iso-solar in form.

If you look at your calendar or date book, you can see what date is indicated as you begin reading. Unless you live in a place where you can remain completely out of touch with the everyday world, you are probably using a Gregorian calendar date. This calendar, named for Pope Gregory XIII (1582 A.D.), completely dismisses or ignores the cycles of the Moon as they relate to our concept of time, except for the computation of religious holidays.

The Gregorian reform adapted aspects of both the Julian and Islamic calendars, attempting to correct the errors of the longstanding Julian system. Almost as drastic in its approach to rectifying calendar errors as the Julian corrections were in 46 B.C.E., the Gregorian system dropped ten days from the calendar on October 5, 1582, declaring it to be October 15th! This was done to restore the equinox to its proper time, which was maintained by the addition of an intercalary day every four years. (However, centennial years are not leap years unless they are precisely divisible by four.)

Although it ignores the lunar patterns completely, the Gregorian calendar is accurate to within approximately twenty-six seconds as it relates to the solar year. This slight difference will increase every 100 years by .53, due to the gradual shortening of the solar year. All this really means is that in one hundred years, that inaccuracy will mount to a whopping 39.78 seconds — not a major concern!

The Gregorian calendar reinforced the decision made in the Council of Nicaea (325 B.C.E.) which determined that Easter, the most important Christian holiday, would be celebrated on the Sunday immediately following the Paschal full Moon (on or after the Vernal Equinox). Thus, the Christian festival of Easter will always fall between March 22 and April 25.

Some German states continued to use the Julian calendar until 1700. Great Britain adopted the Gregorian system in 1752, Russia in 1918, and Turkey in 1927. Most of Europe, however, immediately switched to the new calendar. Evidence of the impact of the changeover can still be seen in some records of the time. Frequent official datemarks included dual dates in an effort to lessen the confusion, such as: November 17/27, 1582.

Calendar Reform

Efforts are frequently made to eliminate the defects of the Gregorian Calendar and establish fixed dates for all festivals and days of rest. Two major revisions, the International Fixed Calendar and the World Calendar, have been presented for consideration, but despite these new systems' vocal proponents, the Gregorian calendar still holds sway.

The International Fixed Calendar proposes a year of thirteen 28-day months. It is basically a perpetual Gregorian calendar in which Sunday begins each month, and every month ends on a Saturday. The extra day is intercalated following December 28, and Leap Day follows June 28; neither day carries a month or weekday name. The thirteenth month, Sol, is intercalated between June and July.

The World Calendar divides the year into 91-day quarters with three months of thirty-one, thirty, and thirty days respectively. Each quarter (January 1, April 1, July 1, October 1) begins on a Sunday, but the months within that quarter begin on other days. The extra day falls at the end of December but has no month or day designation. Leap Day occurs at the end of June and is also separate from the usual month and day indicators.

The current Gregorian calendar needs no improvement in its accuracy related to the solar cycles. However, the predictability of fixed festival or celebration dates, as in the Julian calendar, has distinct advantages. Each of the suggested reforms has vocal proponents, but no extensive support across the general populace. Until the people decide they want a different method of measuring and recording time and events, the vagaries of the Gregorian system will continue to mark the footsteps of time.

Most of us will agree that 1988 (Gregorian) was an eventful year. Portions of our population assigned a different number to that year according to their own calendar. Depending on the time of year, an official entry in Egyptian civil records might have indicated the year 6233. A record-keeper in a synagogue could have noted the date of a Bar Mitzvah for the year 5748 or 5749. A proud family in the Orient may have sent a birth announcement specifying a day and month in the Year of the Rabbit or the Year of the Dragon. A Muslim marriage ceremony would have been recorded as occurring in the year 1366 or 1367.

Each of the dates used in the preceding paragraph is accurate and valid, as it accords with the patterns of time-keeping used by each respective culture. There is a similar pattern of differences in the various predictions of the end of the Age (or World) as we know it. Many authors and researchers have presented varying approaches to this date that are related to the influence of their calendars.

A Christian or Christian mystic studies the prophecies in the Book of

Revelation (New Testament) and considers that end to be nearing quickly. Another believer recognizes that nine of the predictions of Vishnu have been realized, notes that the tenth is becoming reality, and expects it to be evident within the next three decades. Students of Nostradamus state that the end of the world will occur in 2010. According to the Mayan Long Count Calendar, there is no time after Winter Solstice, December 21, 2012. The Sacred Calendar of the Aztecs ended the Fifth World on August 16, 1987 (Harmonic Convergence), with no indication of a possible Sixth World.

There have been doomsdayers and dispensers-of-the-dismals throughout recorded time. Any of the dates given may well be accurate. What we do not truly know is whether the "End" they prophecy is the termination of an age or era or of our physical world. We have only the Now. All any of us can do is to examine our actions each day, live the day as fully we can, and to plan and hope for a positive and productive future to the best of our ability. We can't wash tomorrow's dirty dishes today, but we can plan the meals.

Perhaps we Pagans and Witches have an advantage. We remember Pandora! No matter what occurs, there is Hope. An old adage states, "Where there is Life, there is Hope." We might add, "*and* there is Love." Each of these is a timeless quality. We remember the myths such as Pandora's tale and also remember the Goddess. We know that with every ending comes a new beginning, and that each closing door reveals another which can now open. Life-in-death and death-in-life are eternally intertwined cycles of living.

The adult form we wear is different from the toddler who crawled to reach a toy. The toddler did not die to create the adult — only the forms changed, evolved, and grew — but the essential being and soul is unchanged. In the same manner, with the ending of an Age or World, we shall be the same — and yet be more than we were. Time and Nature exist and shall continue as sacred creations of the Deity we all worship, regardless of Name. There will always be those who live in tune with Nature's clock and its measurement of Time.

Time and its record-keeping are not the only areas in which allowance, understanding, and respect for another's viewpoint are needed. Religion is a matter which is very deeply individual. Yet, many people cannot accept or allow for any pattern of faith which is not "just like" their own. Much of this intolerance is a result of lack of knowledge. Not only are most of us unaware of other faiths, but we are woefully ignorant about the antecedents and history of all faiths, including our own. However, the more common reason for the intolerant attitudes is the lack of faith in one's own beliefs and a hidden fear that they might be "wrong." This leads to a fanatic need to have everyone believe as they do.

In the next chapter we will examine some beliefs and patterns of worship from pre-historic beginnings to present-day evolution. Some of these influences on worship relate to various methods of calendar keeping.

Tree Worship Through the Ages

I can remember as a small child gazing in wonder at the huge pecan tree towering over my head. I was unable to climb it without aid and great effort. Over forty years later, that tree still towers far above me, with no apparent change in the difference of our sizes. Even now, it awes me. I can clasp a limb and swing up into its leafy expanse by myself, but it still requires a significant expenditure of energy to wander through its branches.

The childhood home nearby has been remodeled several times, and the small guest house which once nestled beneath it has fallen and been removed. The vehicles which park in its shade at family reunions are far different from the models which stopped there in years gone by.

However, the tree ignores these changes. Its lifeblood rises in the spring, and its leaves conceal nests perched precariously here and there. The leaves speak with the summer winds and then fall to the ground as winter nears. Each harvest sustains another generation of the squirrels which have been sheltered in its strength. In comparison, I grow older (though not always wiser) and feel the movement of the years. The tree, old and stately when I came to notice it, will outlast me. It will murmur with the winds about the children of the children of the child who played there long ago and comes to play no more. My life may be contained in that whisper of the wind, but the tree is eternal.

Human beings are worshipful by nature. We know in our hearts of our frailties and the swiftness of our lives. In that knowledge we reach beyond ourselves to find that which is greater than the individual. We seek that supreme force or authority which understands and can explain that which we fear and those concepts beyond our comprehension. We seek for Deity.

Ancient man, lacking the burdens of our sophistication and degrees in psychology, found and worshipped that deific presence in the lofty denizens of the forests of his world. Those of us who grew up in one of the Christian sects will remember from our reading of the scriptures the frequent mentions of the Cedars of Lebanon. This tree was held in high regard and worshipped as holy. It was, in essence, the high holy tree of the culture which spawned Christianity. In culture after culture, age after age, the human soul has responded to the spirit of the trees, questioning, and has been answered.

Perhaps the most famous Tree Oracle is Delphi, which centered around a laurel. Romans went to a hillside grove of ilex for their prophecies and predicted the deaths of Domitian and Nero from a dying cypress and laurel. Oak groves near Dodona that were sacred first to the Goddess and then to the Zeus of invading cultures seem to have survived two millenia. Records from Persia, Armenia, and Arabia indicate the significance of oracular trees in those civilizations. The omen sticks of the Druids and willow rods of the Scythian people were used in divination. Divining rods made of mistletoe, fruit trees, willow, rowan, blackthorn, and hazel were and still are used to locate metals, treasures, underground water, oil pockets, ley lines and vortexes.

Symbols of authority and security, such as the staffs carried by military generals through the ages, a policeman's nightstick, scepters held by royalty, and the herald's wand, were an outgrowth of divining instruments formed from those trees. Even the fairy wand which bestowed such finery on Cinderella is an extension of the ageless belief that trees were not only sacred, but were also the source of all wisdom and life.

Modern people of Judeo-Christian upbringing merely show their ignorance of their own holy scriptures when they refer to any form of divination as the "devil's work." Many Hebraic and Christian practices, including the worship of trees and the reverence for divination, were absorbed from the earlier pagan cultures. The Old Testament abounds in references to oracular trees. The signal of a mulberry tree allowed David to attack the Philistines. Scriptures refer to a tree of "the revealers" and the "tree of the diviners," and in other ways emphasize the sacredness of cedars, cypress, and many other trees.

The veneration of trees as deities or as the dwelling place of gods is common to almost every culture. At one time or another, the sycamore fig of Egypt sheltered Osiris, god of the dead, and also Hathor, the mother goddess. These trees were believed to grow at the boundaries of the vast desert and the afterworld. It was said that the deities of those trees gave sustenance to the departing soul as it traveled to the next world. Temples and record cylinders of Assyria and Chaldea showed stylized trees. Later artists would depict those trees as cypress, palm, or pomegranate trees. Even in general literature, the pomegranate is a Tree of Passage.

There are unlimited references in sacred writings to the holy groves and their altars. In the Christian Old Testament, the conflict is evident between the limited monotheistic god and the multiple gods that grew in every forest or grove. The history of the Christian (Catholic) church is rife with the destruction of sacred groves and the older Earth religions and the construction of monasteries and churches upon those holy sites. However, when the new churches and temples were built, symbols of the trees were included in the decorations within them, and their veneration still was evident in very subtle ways.

The true symbolism behind the children's religious song about Zaccheas' climbing the sycamore is easier to understand in this context. Of course he expected to see the "Lord" there — the gods resided in trees! With study we realize that the song is about the *sycamore fig*, guardian of the approach to the afterworld, and not the sycamore as we traditionally think of it in North America. This tale is oriented to a part of the world where for centuries a common image has existed of the souls of the dead climbing the trees, the home of the gods, to reach paradise.

Evidence exists throughout the world — and across many cultures and times — of the practice of tree burials. Instead of a grave inserted into the earth, the limbs of the trees were the final resting place for the departed soul. This practice is easy to comprehend if those trees are the residences of the gods and the trunks are the pathway to the rewarding afterlife. The custom among some of the Plains Indians is more easily understood in this light: where there were no trees large enough to support the weight of the body and its acoutrements, an elevated platform was built to represent the tree, and the burial rites were completed in the traditional manner. Other reasons for the platform burials evolved, but they were originally responses to the inability to effect a tree burial on the open plains.

Trees have been significant in virtually all faiths throughout history. Palm trees and cherubs, common decoration in Assyrian and Babylonian temples, were present in Ezekiel's vision as told in the Christian Old Testament. A bo-tree oversaw Buddha's enlightenment; the cypress, a symbol of the Goddess, was sacred in Persia; and devotees gathered and hung garlands on various sacred trees in India.

Belief in sacred trees was not limited to the more prolific forested areas of the southern climates. The

Buddha under the bo-tree.

wisdom of Odin, passed down in the sacred oral traditions of Nordic Pagans, came from the ash tree. Its twigs formed the runes of the alphabet — not only a means of communication and recording, but also a source for holy knowledge. Some theorists suggest that the source of Odin's runes was not the ash but the yew, since the yew emits a hallucinogenic vapor in its groves. That concept, researchers say, could well have resulted in a loss of time awareness and the subsequent visions which produced the runes.

It is a simple step from revering the trees and their spirits or gods to transferring that sacredness to their surroundings. Prisoners garlanded a holy cypress grove with their chains, as it was a sanctuary from routine forms of justice. The Furies could not touch Orestes while he rested beneath the laurel which was sacred to Apollo. This belief continues today, in many areas, even in defiance of modern laws written to prevent the practice. A prisoner or fugitive has the subtle, unstated right to seek sanctuary from common law in a church (holy ground). The refuge offered by the building today is an outgrowth of such structures built in and on the holy grounds of the sacred Pagan groves. The original reason for the "safe ground" has been forgotten, but the practice remains active in many areas of the world today. The pervasive strength in this belief is subtly evident in our own government. Even a cursory examination of the first amendment to the Bill of Rights and the doctrine of the separation of church and state reveals the shadowy roots of ancient Pagan groves as sacred ground.

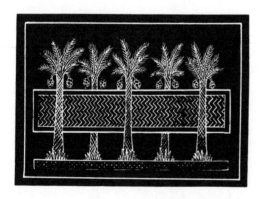

Date Palm and Pond, symbols of abundance and peace, from an ancient Egyptian mural.

Branches, flowers, or fruit removed from sacred trees continued to carry the holiness and sanctity of the tree within. Branches of willow and palm, and leafy branches with fruit, were part of the Hebraic Feast of the Tabernacle, according to scriptural instruction. Following those directions would result in joy in the presence of the Lord. Worshippers brought laurel to the Temple of Apollo. In Greece, the symbol of fertility, the laurel or olive, was decorated with the fruits of the harvest and strips of fabric, much as tinsel and ornaments adorn an evergreen during modern Yule.

Throughout history, trees have been common symbols of fertility. Modern brides carry a bouquet of flowers and greenery. This stems back to early observances of May Day and the carrying of ivy, vine, myrtle, oak, hazel, and hawthorn by brides to insure the fruitfulness of their marriages.

The pine and pine cone as symbols of fertility today can be traced to rituals in Mesopotamia. The priesthood or the ruler would fertilize or cross-pollinate the date palm (their primary food source) by hand in order to promote a good harvest. The resemblance of the male flower of the palm to the pine cone established the cone as both a phallic symbol and an emblem of fertility which later extended to the pine tree itself. In another mythos, Attis, born of an almond, was imprisoned by Cybele in a pine tree only to be reborn from it each spring. In another legend, a pine log imprisoned Osiris, who was released when the log was burned the following year. Comparison can be made between the pine tree and the mountain heather, which some ascribe to Osiris. However, neither the pine nor the heather were indigenous to Egypt. The assignment of either of these trees to Osiris is based on deific qualities similar to those of gods of other cultures, to whom the pine and heather were sacred or relevant. The connection may have been made by invading peoples to whom those trees were familiar.

Worship of trees, whether they still thrived in a grove or were cut down and placed elsewhere as a symbol, continued in many forms. May Day (Beltane, May 1st), a fertility rite, was celebrated throughout Europe and Britain into the 1700's, despite its being prohibited by one Parliament in 1644. The practice has been revived and is in use today, centered around a standing phallic symbol, the Maypole, which was originally a sacred tree specifically cut and placed for that festival purpose.

Still older was the raising of the Djed Pillar, a sacred phallic symbol of ancient Egypt. In extensive ceremonies each year, the vast pillar was raised from the ground and placed upright to signify the strength of the Pharaoh and the duration of his administration. The traditional burning of the Yule Log reflects the concepts of sacrifice and rebirth associated with tree worship. The modern custom of Christmas trees during the holiday season are the evolution of the extension of tree worship to upright posts or pillars as symbols of the sacred trees. Modern Christian opponents of the Pagan movement are, unknowingly, more correct than they know when they scathingly refer to Christmas as a "pagan holiday." They simply forget to mention that they stole it.

Reverence for trees, with the trunk seen as its major part, was extended to any form which symbolized that shape. In some primitive areas, an altar would be placed before an upright tree trunk, whether it was still rooted and growing or not. Ancient Phoenician stones placed upright may well have evolved from that concept, as did the menhirs and standing stones of the British Isles and Brittany. The great ancient pillars of iron found in India — which are still rust-free today after thousands of years — are also facets of this extension of tree worship.

Since all plant forms seemed to grow and survive with or without man, each was considered to contain a deity or at least a spirit. Thus, the knowledge of the plant devas was a most important part of the practices related to herbs. The female spirits of the trees (the nymphs or dryads) were mates to the silvani or fauns such as Pan. The life of the tree was bound to the life of the nymph who resided in it, dying when she did.

Aphrodite left the baby Aeneas with the dryads. Daphne escaped Apollo by becoming a laurel. Other connections in mythology have been made between Helike (Helice, Hecate) and the willow, as well as between Rhea and the pomegranate, Philyra and the linden or lime tree, and Athene and the olive. Depending on where she was worshipped, Artemis was the goddess of the myrtle, cedar, laurel, willow, or the hazel. Even the founding of Rome is said to have occurred where the roots of a fig tree that extended into the Tiber river stopped the cradle in which Remus and Romulus floated. In another mythology, Philemon and Baucis were turned into an oak and a linden, respectively, at their deaths because of their love for each other. The two trees grew so near each other that the branches could intertwine. Just as Philemon and Baucis had loved and held each other in life, the branches of the oak and the linden intertwined and held each other close.

Daphne escaped Apollo by becoming a laurel tree.

Because of the belief that a spirit resided there, the ancients felt it was bad luck to cut down a tree. It was a serious offense for many years throughout much of the British Isles to fell certain trees; especially the rowan, birch, hawthorn, or oak. The crime was punishable by death.

By legend, a tree would bleed when it was cut. However, cutting a branch from an elder tree (a tree in which witches purportedly lived) would instead supposedly result in the injury to the arm of some elderly woman in the area. This belief appears to be of a later origin, possibly evolving from the time of the persecutions, when witches first were designated as negative or evil beings even while recognized as being in their harmony with nature and with growing things. Prior to that time, such women were revered as Wise Women or Elders, just as the Elder tree was sacred to the Goddess in her aged aspect.

It is unlikely that any country or culture exists today that does not have legends of spirits, elves, pixies, fairies or such which reside in trees. Folk tales of Germanic and Scandinavian countries refer to the Moss Women or Moss People. Other examples include the wood demon of Russia, a wood ghost in South America which beckons men to their death, and the wood spirit of Japan with a hawk's head and a man's body.

As late as the second century of our Common Era, Maximus of Tyr wrote of the dressing of trees in the garden to represent Dionysus at the time of that god's festival. Even today, in many Eastern countries, gifts are brought to and clothing is hung on the sacred trees as a means of bringing good health and luck to the giver.

The concept of the tree as a deity expanded to become the concept of a tree which contained the universe. Such a tree was rooted deeply in the earth and thus was privy to the knowledge of the underworlds. It spread its branches in the skies and contained all that exists. The World Tree, Yggdrasil, is Scandinavian. The Qabbala (Hebrew mysticism) focuses on the Tree of Life, a three-pillared, ten-branched universe, with its branches forming the positive world and its attributes; its roots become the equally complete but negative tree. Asvattha, the Fig, is the World Tree in India. The Tooba tree is the paradise tree of the Koran. Even in the more modern Grecian legends, Hercules conquered the guardian of the sacred tree and took the fruits of that tree, the apples of knowledge. The World-Pillar of the Saxons, a tree trunk which exemplified their basic beliefs, was destroyed by Emperor Charlemagne to indicate his conquest of that culture. In the southwestern United States, trees in desolate areas are said to have been the sites for the entrances used by the Anasazi to journey to and from the third world and this one.

Trees were revered due to the nature of the gods who resided in them or to whom each tree was sacred, or because of aspects of the tree's own nature.

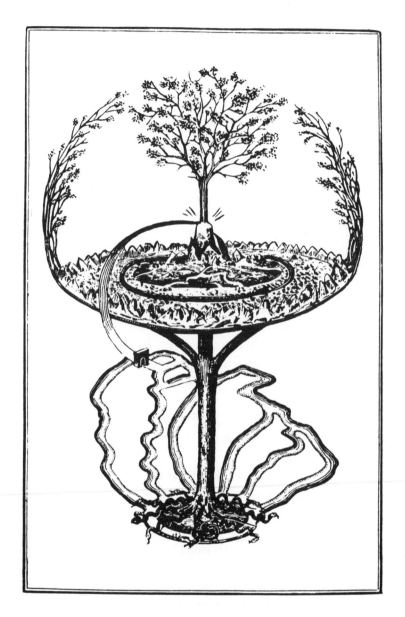

Yggdrasil, from Finn Magnusen's EDDALAEREN
Copenhagen, 1824

The ash, for example, supposedly protected one from drowning. Along with the ash, other trees such as the hazel, oak, willow, and rowan were honored for their divinatory traits. In addition to the above, trees which were prized for their defensive qualities against evil included the hawthorn and birch. Mistletoe protected the home against fire, and the birch or rowan guarded the man or woman who carried it and kept the livestock safe when it was attached to their barn or shelter. Lightning would not harm the individual who carried the oak, olive, elm, holly, or bay laurel. On the North American continent, the pinon pines were revered by the American Indians as a source of food.

Legends exist in many cultures to indicate that humankind originated with the trees. Nordic myth tells of two seashore trees which changed into the man and woman from whom all of Earth's population came. In Greek myth, humankind was produced from the seeds of trees. In some Oriental faiths it is believed that one's ancestors return to this life in the form of plants and trees which thus become sacred and are not to be wantonly picked or destroyed.

Within the race consciousness of humankind is the awareness of the deific nature of trees and our relationship with them. From this belief evolved the common practice of planting a tree when a child is born. In some cultures, observing the growth of the tree gave the family indications of the future progress of the child. In earlier times, the tree was planted on what would one day become that child's portion of the family property. As it grew, it became the meeting place to which members of their family would return for councils and family decisions. The family thus took its symbolism, and sometimes its name, from that family tree. A simple perusal of any telephone book will reveal such names as Oakes, Birch (Burch, or Burke), Birchfield, Greenwood, Roundtree (Rountree, or Rowantree), Ash (Ashe or Asche), Grove, Hawthorn(e), Longtree, Woods, and others — all of which are remnants of the veneration and worship of trees in times past.

Modern people are intelligent and not given to ruling their lives by superstitions. More logical than primitive peoples of the past, we know that a god doesn't live in a tree house (or even a tree), that a tree cannot comprise the totality of the universe, and that wood nymphs and satyrs only exist in legend and myth — or do we?

As Pagans, we know that the forces of nature and a level of the consciousness of life exists in all living things. Today, we respect and revere that life without perhaps deifying the moss by the stream or the majestic evergreen. We take pride in our family names and are delighted when a casual search of genealogical records indicates that someone special, famous, or memorable might lie in direct lineage on our family tree. We celebrate May Day, decorate a Christmas tree, kiss under the mistletoe, "knock on wood," and pride ourselves on our modern superiority, knowledge, and superstitious-free intelligence.

We Pagans may be as unknowledgeable about our faith and spiritual heritage as we observe those of dominant religions are of their own. Unknowingly, we sometimes blindly follow custom, enacting shadow rites of a vaguely remembered reverence. In our modern complacency and faulty memories we may easily miss the knowledge of and joyous interaction with the spirits of the woods and the gods who still dwell in trees.

Perhaps we can find inspiration and an inner knowledge in the rhythm and rhyme of poetic thought, which is said to be the true form of worship. Alfred Joyce Kilmer wrote the following poem for Mrs. Henry Mills Alden approximately three years before his death in France during World War I.

Trees

(For Mrs. Henry Mills Alden, circa 1913)

I think that I shall never see
A poem lovely as a tree.

A tree whose hungry mouth is prest
Against the earth's sweet flowing breast;

A tree that looks at God all day,
And lifts her leafy arms to pray;

A tree that may in summer wear
A nest of robins in her hair;

Upon whose bosom snow has lain
Who intimately lives with rain.

Poems are made by fools like me,
But only God can make a tree.

Alfred Joyce Kilmer

An Overview of the Ogham

On ancient stone menhirs that sometimes stand isolated on a lonely plain or moor, the Ogham runes have been discovered leading up one side, marching across the lintel, and descending the other side, untouched by time. However, they have on occasion been uprooted, turned upside-down by those who came along afterward, and re-engraved with the Christian god-names which that later culture worshipped.

The variable readings of these ancient runes has led to the differences you will find in discussions and use of the Ogham. Historians disagree as to what form its use should take, but they do seem in consensus that it is a left-to-right alphabet. The significant point to remember is that the left end of the base or horizontal line of writing will always be turned upward to form the top of the vertical. If the line of runes followed the up-across-and-down outline of the menhirs, they are read from lower left upward to the lintel, left-to-right across the lintel itself, and then down the right vertical row.

Thus, the phrase "The Ogham Alphabet" could be written in either of the two forms illustrated here — which are identical except for the reading angle and direction used. It can still be as easily read vertically as horizontally.

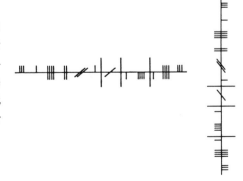

In this volume you will frequently find mention of the Ogham or a reference to an "Oghmic" characteristic. Although this is not a linguistic or historical treatise on ancient alphabets, some awareness of the Ogham is necessary to fully understand this study of the sacred trees. In addition, the use of a particular glyph, rune, or alphabet character is vital to the specific ritual format shared here. Therefore, let us look briefly at what the references and connections will be.

When a discussion arises related to the Ogham, you are as apt to find passions or tempers rising as you are likely to hear a calm discussion. One person in the group may refer to it as a "pre-historic alphabet" and another may take exception, saying that if it was pre-historic, then it existed prior to written records and thus an alphabet would not exist. To one follower of Oghmic studies, it is totally an Irish topic; to the person sitting next to him or her, it might be thought Druidic, or simply a Celtic influence which pervaded the British Isles, and not attributable to any single culture.

Each of these viewpoints is correct to some extent. Ogham alphabet characters have been found on isolated monoliths which date as far back as 4,500 B.C.E., which indicates six-and-a-half millenia of use. This certainly qualifies the alphabet as having been in use earlier than most written records and histories found to date, other than pictograph writings of pre-dynastic Egypt (5,500 B.C.E.).

However, the history of mankind, especially in the areas which include Ireland and surrounding cultures, was handed down from generation to generation by oral tradition, which existed long before the remainder of the world thought to record it in concrete form. At the same time, the Ogham was considered a signal, cipher, or hand alphabet used for silent communication at semi-close distances, perhaps like the "fan-talk" of young ladies of Russia in years gone by. In the use of the Ogham as a hand-cipher, fingers of either hand were used with the bridge of the nose as the center or dividing line that we are accustomed to seeing today in the written form of Ogham.

One of the fascinating facets of the Ogham is its use as a basic primer alphabet. As confusing and out-of-sequence as it appears at first glance, the system and pattern of the Ogham can be easily grasped by a child who has had no exposure to alphabets. Utilizing the Ogham as a pre-primer before teaching the traditional Roman alphabet we use today is an intriguing experiment in teaching the written language.

The Ogham alphabet characters themselves resemble nothing so much as a collection of hash marks very similar to some rank designations in many armed services. However, the Ogham characters are much more easily mastered and remembered. The set of Ogham runes or glyphs is composed of thirteen consonants: B, L, N, F, S, H, D, T, C, M, Ng, G, and R, each of which also represents a specific Moon month and its sacred tree. In addition, there are five vowel trees — A, O, U, E, and I — which separate the year into respective seasons. These seasons are Rebirth (A), Spring (O), Summer (U),

B ┤	H ├	M ╲	A ┼
L ╡	D ╞	G ╳	O ╪
N ╧	T ╟	Ng ╳	U ╪
F ╤	C ╠	SS ╳	E ╪
S ╪	Q ╠	R ╳	T ╪
		Y ╪ : ╪	

The Ogham Alphabet with the Beth-Luis-Nion Sequence

Autumn (E), and Death (I). The extra day of the year — the day following the Winter Solstice — is assigned to the Mistletoe. Its letter is the double-I (Y, or J). It is this sequence of nineteen trees (plus a few other ideas) that we will use as our focus for the rituals contained in this book.

Before we examine the trees, however, let's examine the differences between the lunation (Moon pattern) and the Moon-month. Beginning on the second day following the Winter Solstice, the thirteen Moon-months begin, each with a 28-day cycle which repeats through the seasons, year after year. However, the actual timing and dates for the New or Full Moon will vary from one annual cycle to the next. In one specific year, a New Moon may occur immediately following the Winter Solstice. The following year at that time might be a Full Moon, or there may be no lunation celebration point at all until after January begins. During one annual lunar cycle there will be thirteen New Moons and twelve Full Moons; in the next, the pattern is likely to be reversed. Often, the last New Moon of the year may be celebrated at its Full Moon point as the first Moon of the new year. This adjustment is due to the slight overlap in lunar cycles.

Because of this factor, many groups choose to adjust their celebration time to focus on either the New Moon or the Full Moon, depending upon which portion of the lunation provides thirteen actual points for ritual observance through the year.

Other groups may choose to gather for worship only at the Full Moon and will combine two Moons somewhere within the year. The thirteenth Moon is frequently designated for a selected date prior to the solstice, rather than marking a true day of lunation. This point will be explained more thoroughly later on in the book.

Some students or practitioners of magic use the Ogham as a magical alphabet in which to keep their personal written records of working or their Book of Lights and Shadows. Those who tend to be skilled at spelling words in general may experience a slight difficulty in using it until they become accustomed to it (just as those who are native speakers of English tend to constantly misspell Spanish as they begin learning it, because Spanish is phonetically consistent with no diphthongs, silent characters, or overuse of double letters). If spelling has never been your best talent, then you'll love using the Ogham! Just write what you have to say the way it sounds.

For example, consider the difference between the voiced and aspirated sound sets of either "B" and "P," or "V" and "F". The distinction between them is whether they are voiced or only aspirated. Try saying just those letter sounds; you will find that the "B" and "V" are more vocalized, with a "heavier" sound, and that the "P" and "F" are more of a whispered utterance. Focus your attention on the feel of your lips as you say them. "B" and "P" start with the same position. With "B" the lips meet and separate somewhat as the sound is completed. With the sound of "P," the difference is in the aspiration and in a slightly wider and sharper separation of the lips to allow for that passage of aspirated air. A similar pattern occurs with the "V" and "F," except that the upper teeth meet the bottom lips to begin the sound. The difference again lies in the aspiration or voiced quality and in a minimal increase in the separation of the lips to complete the sound.

Yes, I know . . . you bought this book because you wanted to know about the sacred Druidic trees, not because you wanted a layman's lesson in linguistics! Bear with me a moment; I am presuming that you are interested in being able to effectively use the alphabet as well as the ritual and mythological aspects of the knowledge. That brings us back to why this was introduced in the first place.

The Ogham is written phonetically. Similarities in the voiced and aspirated sounds will eliminate some of the letters you are accustomed to using in writing Roman characters or in speaking American English. For example, "Carol" begins with the letter "Coll," which is a "K" sound; and "Cindy" uses the initial letter "Saille," or the "S" sound. "Fearn," the "F" sound, serves double duty as the "V," and the aspirated "P" is represented by "Beth" (B). Later Ogham alphabets may include a letter for each aspiration, but those glyphs or runes are not contained in the form of the Ogham used here.

In your magical working with the Ogham, spelling well will not be as great a concern as being able to simplify the sounds you commit to paper and your ability to tune into and harmonize with the mood and movement of that Moon and its tree.

Many books provide a scholarly treatise on the Ogham and related topics. However, a basic overview, as suggested in the title of the chapter, is all that is needed here. Therefore, let's finish the skeleton or framework on which you will begin building your use of this magical alphabet, so that you can begin fleshing it out in your practice.

Ogham is divided into several "flights" or sets of letters which have similar characteristics. The first set — B, L, N, F, and S — are short "hash marks" placed to the left of or below the base line but not passing through the center. Thus, "B" has only one mark, "L" has two, and each successive letter has one more mark to the left of or below the line than did the one before it. Respectively, the letter names and their trees are: Beth (Birch), Luis (Rowan), Nion (Ash), Fearn (Alder), and Saille (Willow).

B ⊣
L ⊣
N ⊣
F ⊣
S ⊣

H ⊢
D ⊢
T ⊢
C ⊢
Q ⊢

The second flight is also formed by short marks which do not cross the center or base line; but these letter-runes are placed above or to the right of that line. Included in this flight are: H, D, T, C, and Q. These letters also are formed in patterns of one to five stroke marks sequentially. They are Huath (Hawthorn), Duir (Oak), Tinne (Holly), Coll (Hazel), and Quert (Wild Apple).

Although simple arithmetic suggests that there are ten trees indicated to this point, we have really only covered nine of the traditional Moon trees. The Hazel is the tree for the ninth Moon, and Quert, the Wild Apple, is not normally used. I would suggest using them together. However, if you are a purist by nature, eliminate the Wild Apple (Q) and use only the Hazel for the ninth Moon's tree. In my personal research and ritual practice I found that they belong together in the same Moon, much as the Blackthorn and Whitethorn (forms of Hawthorn) in different parts of the year are adjacent to each other in the hand (they are close because they deal with the two aspects of magic: negative and positive). With the Hazel and Wild Apple, the commonality is immortality: attained through wisdom, or through inspiration.

The third and final flight of the consonant trees contains only four letters in common usage. Muin-M, Gort-G, Ngetal-Ng, and Ruis-R. Each of these runes is formed by slanted marks which completely cross the central or base line. The Blackthorn (Straiff-SS or Z) is sometimes included in this flight, which gives the thirteenth tree, Ruis (Death or Journey Tree) five strokes. They are drawn across the vertical base line in a downward slant from upper left to lower right. On the horizontal baseline they are placed from lower left to upper right. The names and trees assigned to these letters are, respectively, Muin (Vine), Gort (Ivy), Ngetal (Reed), Straiff (Blackthorn), and Ruis (Elder).

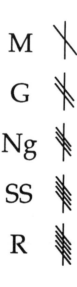

M

G

Ng

SS

R

The remaining letter-runes are the vowels that were sacred to and reserved for the Goddess. They mark the stations of the Wheel of the Year. These are formed by straight strokes that cross the center line and lie equally on either side of it. They are drawn across the vertical center line or are upright on the horizontal baseline. That sequence is A, O, U, E, and I. Study indicates the Mistletoe as the sixth, the double II (Y or J). The vowel trees are:

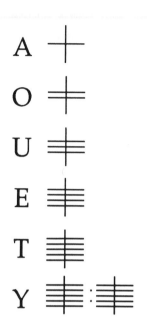

Ailm is the silver fir, the birth tree of Winter Solstice. Onn is the name of the Goddess of Spring and is symbolic of the Furze or Gorse. Ura, the Heather, is the mid-summer tree. Eadha, the White Poplar or Aspen, is the tree of autumn equinox. The traditional final vowel-tree is Idha (Yew), the death tree of midwinter or winter solstice. The sixth tree is the Mistletoe (J or Y), which is the Extra Day of the Year, the day following the rebirth of the Sun. The work I have done with II, the Mistletoe, is purely speculative and experiential. However, its validity in magical work appears to be borne out in practice.

With a basic grounding in the Tree System on which we focus this approach to lunar worship patterns, it is easy to move on to put the trees, the letters, the Moons, and the mythologies together in ritual or meditative practice. Before we do, however, let's analyze a generic ritual to see how it flows together, and try to understand the ways in which we can fit our tree-knowledge into a comfortable ritual pattern.

For more material on the Ogham, turn to the appendices at the back of this book, which contain a Correspondence Chart and supplemental notes on the trees. It is suggested, however, that you read through the rituals in order before perusing the correspondences or general information. The intent, focus, and impact of each ritual will have a greater meaning for you if you "experience" it first. Use your logic to determine why it had a significance for you *after* there is an effect to consider.

Find yourself a quiet space and relax. Light a candle if you wish, and let's share the ritual of the Great Tree as a prelude to a season of trees and a year of Moons.

"Let's try it . . . this way . . ."

The Great Tree

TEMPLE IS PREPARED:
CIRCLE IS CAST:
DEDICATION:

The great forces of the universe gathered. The God and Goddess joined in thought to create for their Children a symbol of their unity and harmony to be visible when the children were unable to see the Mother-Father. They joined in love and began their work.

DRAWING DOWN THE LUMINARIES:

High Priestess (HPS): *To show our unity in love, the symbol we create must have a single force to be seen. Our Children will know that they, too, are One within Us.*

(High Priest (HP) & HPS "build" a tree trunk and set it in place in the circle)

HP: *Within that symbol must be the image of our passage through the year.*

HPS: *Its beginning, midpoint, and its ending. . .*

(HPS adds a double "branch")

HP: *Its points of balance and equality.*

(HP adds a double branch)

HPS: *There must be joy within it, and times of celebration: of my return from birthing you, and of the bounty of our harvest.*

(HPS adds a double branch)

HP: *And celebration of my virile strength and our guardianship of our Children's souls.*

(HP adds a double branch)

EARTH: *May we, the elements, aid in this creation? I offer a season of quiet and rest, a time of knowing the inner self — as the Earth rests in winter.*

(Earth places a skeletal branch at the North)

29

FIRE: *I offer a season of stirring and growth, a time to stretch the inner self and reach to new potentials — as the Sun warms the seeds of earth to life.*

(Fire places a branch with "new" leaves on it)

WATER: *I offer a season of fullness of growth — a time for life and joy — as the rains of the year encourage the need to grow.*

(Water places a branch covered with leaves at the West)

AIR: *I offer a season of change: a time to celebrate past growth and prepare for a time of inner silence, as the winds bring scents of both harvest and decay to our lives.*

(Air places a branch to the East with scattered, colored leaves and fruit shapes)

HPS: *Ah, yes! And its roots shall be able to reach deep within me, the Earth Mother, for nourishment and stability.*

(HPS unrolls "roots" attached to base of trunk)

HP: *Within that unity must also be the vision of the differences within us so that the scope of existence is not limited. The branches shall reach to the skies, and I shall give them strength.*

(HP extends ribbons attached to various branches to reach each participant.)

HPS: *I am the Weeping Willow. I express the ability of the Goddess to feel deeply and to weep tears of joy or sorrow.*

HP: *I am the Oak. The strength of the Sun God, the Sky Father, is seen in me.*

Participant 1: *I am the Maple. The inner sweetness of life, the union of the God and Goddess can be tasted in the sap I bring in the spring.*

Part. 2: *I am the Pecan. In my shade is symbolized the shelter found in the love of the Mother-Father. I provide food for the body as they give food for the soul.*

Part. 3: *I am the Pine. I am sacred to the God and show his gentler side. I am ever green and growing, as is His compassion.*

Part. 4: *I am the Cedar, symbol of the Goddess. I am the pleasurable scent of purification, and protection from unpleasantries. I, too, am green throughout the year, as the presence of the Goddess is always with you.*

HP: *Let us take a moment to examine our roots, the depths to which they reach, the movement of our branches in the skies, and how we each reflect the Great Tree in our growth.*

MEDITATION TIME:

HPS: *Remember the All that you are in your thoughts, which are your branches piercing the skies.*

(Air symbol is shared around the circle)

HP: *In the expression of your energies is your growth, the reflection of the Great Tree which others see within you.*

(Fire symbol is shared)

HPS: *Remember as your love flows that it is the life-force within you, the sap which expresses the sweetness of life.*

(Water symbol is shared)

HP: *In the dedication and surety of where you stand, remember from whence you came and the source of your strength, and your roots to the past which enable your future.*

(Earth symbol is shared)

HPS: *May we grow as the trees in the forest, each beautiful in our own way. . .*

HP: *Our roots reaching into the same rich earth . . .*

HPS: *Our branches reaching to the same bright sky.*

HP: *May we each grow to our full beauty from the seed we now are.*

(HP gives each participant a seed)

CHANT IS BEGUN: *"The God — He is alive! Magic is afoot! The Goddess is a Tree! Her Magic is in Me!"*

HPS: *We are united in our strength and faith, yet we can delight in our differences, which reflect the All in all.*

THANKS TO THE DEITIES:
DISMISSAL OF SPIRITS:
CIRCLE IS ENDED:

Analysis of the Great Tree Ritual

In this chapter we will take apart the preceding ritual little by little, with explanations of why "this" is done here in one particular manner, and why something else is done in a different way elsewhere. For those of you who are experienced in sharing or conducting rituals, this section may offer little of interest other than insight into another person's viewpoint.

However, one of the main purposes of this book is to be able to share some of the "little things" that are usually only learned in personal study with a particular teacher or group. Thus, this chapter is really for all of us, and for those questions — spoken or unspoken — that arise in seeing "how someone else does it."

The material in bold type is reprinted from the ritual. Following it in standard type is the commentary on or explanation of that material. It may be a simple statement or clarification; or it may have suggestions and "how-to's" related to items and their sources; or it may describe how to create a specific tool or accessory. I hope it is of some interest and help in its approach. If you are thoroughly familiar with rituals of all kinds but always find something new that is of interest to you, then let's get started.

THE GREAT TREE

I chose this title because the book concerns the sacred trees of the British Isles, and because of an inner image of one great tree which contains all the shapes, leaves, fruits, and knowledge of all the trees, reflecting parts of itself into one tree's pattern of growth and another's form of fruit. It is a title to suggest the unity of All.

TEMPLE IS PREPARED:

Even if you are working in a solitary-meditation form of worship, the area where you plan to be needs some preparation. If you are converting a living room or study into a temple for the moment, there may be items that need to be picked up or moved. The floor may need to be swept or vacuumed. You need to gather the items you will require and begin placing them where they should be or where you will be able to reach them at appropriate times. These are physical-level preparations.

If the area has been used for other functions, there may be vibrations that need to be identified or cleared in order to create a serene and undisturbed environment in which to work, worship, or meditate.

The simplest way to clear any area is to visualize a glowing sphere of pure light surrounding it. If you need to visualize a particular color rather than pure light, I would suggest clear or white. See a whirling center of intense light. Allow it to grow and expand to fill that entire globe, pushing any shadow of negativity or improper vibration ahead of it through the outer boundary of the sphere, so that nothing but light remains within that space.

When you have cleaned and cleared the area, have all items to be used in place or within reach, and have established a serene environment or atmosphere for your work, then the Temple is prepared.

CIRCLE IS CAST:

A separate and sacred area is created in which to work or worship. You may draw a circle with chalk, form a visual boundary by putting ritual objects in place, or visualize a sphere of pure light surrounding you and your working area. You will find more information about circle-casting in various books written by Wiccans such as Janet and Stewart Ferrar, Marion Weinstein, Dorene Valiente, Raymond Buckland, Scott Cunningham, and Starhawk. Examine the different methods and find one which works well for you.

DEDICATION:

Whether this is done as part of preparation, or is integral to the opening of the circle and the ritual itself, needs to be quite clear in your mind and inner heart before the ritual begins. A circle can be dedicated to a particular purpose (whatever reason there is for the observance of that rite), or it may be consecrated to a specific deity or set of deities.

For example, suppose there have been some nit-picky little differences or disagreements within the group recently that seem to have hung on and on. This happens with any group, especially in today's world. However, you cannot permit those vibrations to remain, or they will continue to affect in a negative manner all that the group does. In such an instance, the circle might be dedicated to the purpose of Unity, or of Resolution of Differences. If you wish, you could extend the dedication to specifically call on the vibrations and influence of a deity whom you feel most represents harmony and unity.

In another instance, the group might be gathering to work on healing matters. In such a case, the circle might be dedicated simply to Healing, or to Hygiea, Ptah, Jupiter, or other beneficial or healing dieties.

Once that dedication is made, the area should not be used for other purposes until the intended one is completed and the spirits called to it are released.

The great forces of the universe gathered.

Aside from the simple statement to begin the ritual, this sentence sets the feel and imagery in motion to begin gathering strength and momentum.

The God and Goddess joined

Polarity and balance within the circle is also symbolized here, in addition to the obvious meaning. It also sets the direction or source for the work to be done in full view of the deity(ies).

As far as the force of the ritual is concerned, the impact is heightened at this point if the HPS and HP reach, as one, to light the God and Goddess candles together. The physical and visible joining of their hands reinforces the wording and inner image of the ritual. Nothing need be said regarding it; it is simply there reinforcing and underlying all that exists in the rite.

in thought

The total intimacy and unity of being is indicated here. There are no barriers or differences where the meeting and mating of the minds are concerned.

It is also a subtle reminder that what we do within the circle is done in our hearts and minds. All the "trappings" are not needed.

to create

Reflects back to the image of the joining — balanced, polarized — Male and Female, Active and Passive, Outgoing and Receptive, and so forth. Creating, in any sense, is a magical event. In this instance, it is being done by the Gods themselves.

for their Children

Feelings of nurturing, warmth, and caring support are inherent in this brief phrase, which firmly re-establishes the connections we have with the God and Goddess.

a symbol of their unity and harmony

A symbol is an image, idea, or thing which represents much more than words can express and convey. This imagery or symbolism can only be truly experienced and felt within, as can that deific oneness.

to be visible when the Children were unable to see the Mother-Father.

Sometimes we become so bogged down in everyday things that we lose sight of our focus and our goals, as well as our relationship and connection to the Gods.

They joined in love and began their work.

Love is the greatest creative force. What the gods do (As Above) is reflected into our sphere of existence (So Below). They began the work on abstract planes. We continue their work in the manifest planes.

DRAWING DOWN THE LUMINARIES:

I have placed this after the initial statements because the awareness of the presence of the deities on higher planes is needed before the effect of that presence can be called to this plane.

This phrase is more commonly heard or used as "Drawing down the Moon." My personal feeling is that both the God and Goddess aspects are essential. One may be more dominant at one time, the other the next; either may be more oriented to one purpose or another. It is that eternal balance between them for which we strive within and without ourselves.

The physical act of lowering upraised hands as a symbol of bringing those aspects into our circle and ourselves can be felt by the HP and HPS as well as by the members of the working circle, and is completely effective in itself.

However, there may be times when you desire something more expressive and specific. In those instances, a mini-ceremony called the "Wine Blessing" may be what you are looking for. An example of a worded wine blessing is in "Invocations, Oracles, and Responses." The wine blessing can be combined with specific wording or can be effectively done in silence.

Since we each have a masculine and a feminine side or aspect of ourselves, the blessing can be done in a group circle or in a solitary ritual. If solitary, take your athame (ceremonial dagger, an Air tool) and hold it firmly with both hands above the filled chalice. Form the image in your mind of that ultimate union, that of the God and Goddess within. It is basic to the concept of sunlight lancing to the Earth, of the joining of lovers, of Spirit to the Flesh. When that image is clear in your mind, plunge the athame firmly into the Chalice, seeing and feeling that sunlight or Spirit descending into and joining with the Chalice to complete the balanced union.

The same procedure is used in group practice. The group leaders (HPS and HP) each take up one of the elements — that is, the athame or the Chalice — and together form the imagery and complete the symbolic conjoining. You'll find more information about this practice in the chapter on Invocations.

If you prefer to slowly lower the upraised arms, then establish that balance within yourself when solitary, or match your efforts as group leaders. It is quite effective if those leaders turn to face each other for this portion of the ritual. Establish a solid eye-contact with your partner and see him or her as the God or Goddess. Call to that deity in your heart and mind, deeply seeking their presence within yourself and within the circle. While maintaining that visual connection, match the movements of your arms so that the two sets of arms lower in unison. As you do this, clearly envision yourself, the circle, and all within it drawing the qualities of the deities into themselves.

You may wish to utilize a brief God-Goddess chant for the time of that movement. Some deity chants are shared in the appendix of chants in the back of this book.

(NOTE: For the remainder of this analyzing chapter, I will not go into quite so much depth or detail concerning phrases or segments within an area of speech or activity. However, with the earlier examples, you should have no problem picking apart added symbolism and meanings in the paragraphs or sentences that follow.)

HPS: To show our unity in love, the symbol we create must have a single force to be seen. Our Children will know that they, too, are One within Us.

This segment of the ritual sets down specifications and directions to be taken by the deific forces being channeled in creation. At the deepest levels of awareness is the knowledge that we truly are One — with each other and with the Gods — despite any differences in our practice and our approach.

(HP & HPS "build" a tree trunk and set it in place in the circle)

This is the "symbol" of the Oneness of the Gods. Although a tree trunk could be prepared ahead of time and be placed in the circle, much of the impact and momentum would be lost with the absence of the visible and spontaneous creative action.

Following are two possible methods of easily "creating" a tree trunk within the circle space.

Poster Board: This material is available at most novelty or variety stores, supermarkets, and some drug stores. A 21" by 28" sheet can usually be purchased for less than a dollar. You will need two or three sheets. It comes in a variety of colors, thus allowing you to add to the symbolism by using brown sheets for the trunk and green sheets for the "branches."

Roll the sheet so that the ends overlap, and fasten them together. Large paper clips or velcro fastener tabs glued to the edges will do this nicely. You could also pre-cut a slot and a barbed extension at the ends so they can be fitted into each other. If you are artistic and have the time before the ritual, you could paint the sheet to look like bark or have a hollow with a small animal showing — but the simple "trunk" will be adequate.

Pre-cut vertical slots in either end will be the upper portion of the trunk where you can smoothly fit the "branches" into place later. You will have one more addition to the base of the trunk prior to the ritual, but we will discuss that in a moment.

Another method is to use the oversized chenille pipestem cleaners that are 18" to 2 feet in length. These are available in most arts and craft stores. By placing eight of the chenille stems together and twisting them to hold them in place, the tree can be easily created. Begin twisting approximately two inches from the bottom of the collection of stems, and twist upward to within one-third of the total length from the top. This spacing will permit the formation of roots and branches, as indicated in the remainder of the ritual. One great advantage of this method is that the construction will stand by itself on completion, and will look like a tree as you progress through the remainder of the ritual.

HP: Within that symbol must be the image of our passage through the year.

Remember that they were creating something to be visible when the Children could not see the God and Goddess.

HPS: Its beginning, midpoint, and its ending. . .

Yule is both the beginning and the ending — as in the rebirth, then death and rebirth of the Sun. Mid-Summer, between one year's Yule and the next, is the point when the Sun is strongest and brightest.

If you use the chenille stems, simply pull two opposing stems out from the "trunk" so they resemble branches extending in the appropriate places related to the Wheel of the Year.

(HPS adds a double "branch")

This branch can be cut as a wide "U" from the poster board so that its straight bottom edge slides into two pre-cut slots at the "top" of the trunk. See illustration following.

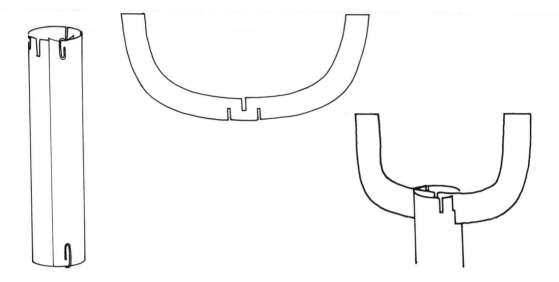

If using the chenille stems, follow similar directions as before, in keeping with the present section of the ritual.

HP: Its points of balance and equality.

The two solar festivals called the Vernal Equinox and Autumnal Equinox are those dates when the day and night are equal in length.

(HP adds a double "branch")

This branch can be cut as a tall "Y" with a short stem and wide arms. It can be pre-cut at the base to overlap the slot in the center of the first (solstice's) branch.

Simply follow the established pattern if using the chenille stems.

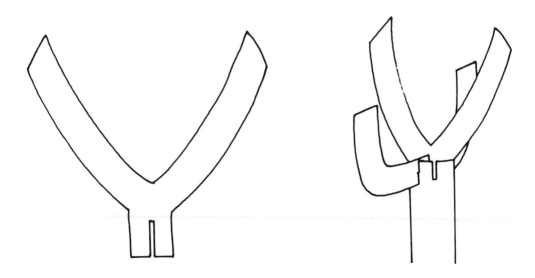

HPS: There must be joy within it, and times of celebration: of my return from birthing you, and of the bounty of our harvest.

The symbolism here is of the cross-quarterly celebrations — (non-solar festival points) in the Wheel of the Year. At Candlemas (February 2nd), the Goddess traditionally returns to Earth from a time of solitude following the birth of the Sun. That Sun-child at maturity is the Sun-King who is Her lover. Lammas (August 1st) is the first of the harvest festivals, celebrating the reaping of the first of the grains, fruits, nuts, and livestock.

(HPS adds a double "branch")

This branch can be a wide, sweeping curve. It should be placed so that its points are between the Yule and Spring branches on one side, and Summer and Autumn on the other.

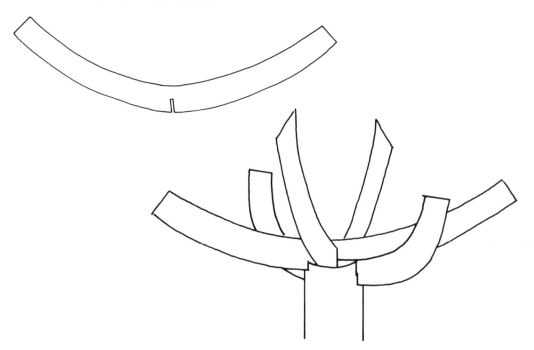

HP: And celebration of my virile strength and our guardianship of our Children's souls.

Beltane, May 1st, is a fertility festival in honor of the return of life to the Earth. The maypole itself is a phallic symbol celebrating the increasing strength and life-giving force of the Sun. Both Beltane and Halomas (Samhain, on October 31) are times when the veil between the world of the spirits and the world of man is the thinnest. At these times, one can reach through the veil, with love, and contact those whom you have loved but who have made transition to the spirit world. At those times, especially at Halomas, the God and Goddess stand guard while we visit with and cherish those we have loved before.

(HP adds a double branch)

This branch fills in the remaining two quadrants in the tree, pointing to the spaces between autumn and Yule, and between spring and summer on the other side. If it is cut as a tall, narrow "Y" with slight curves to the upper points, it will complete the image of the upper branches of a tree.

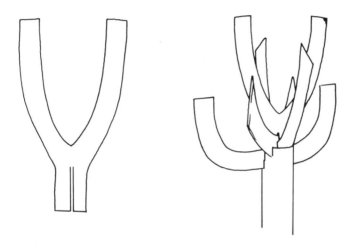

EARTH: May we, the elements, aid in this creation? I offer a season of quiet and rest, a time of knowing the inner self — as the Earth rests in winter.

The Earth season begins with Winter Solstice around the 21-23rd of December. Our bodies, like the Earth, are not as active and we turn more within ourselves.

(Earth places a skeletal branch at the North)

This branch represents the apparent lack of life in this season. If desired, small tufts of torn cotton puffs can be glued to the branch to represent snow. For this symbol, I would suggest a real branch that can be laid at the base of the "Great Tree" on the North.

FIRE: I offer a season of stirring and growth, a time to stretch the inner self and reach to new potentials — as the Sun warms the seeds of the Earth to life.

Spring Equinox marks the beginning of the Fire season, as the Sun moves into Aries, the first sign of the zodiac. At this time in most areas, the indications of life are still slight, and most growth has not leafed out or has minimal first leaves or blossoms. Our bodies are beginning to stir to activity again and expand our activities and ideas. By the end of this season, the warming Sun has promoted full growth, just as the fire of our energies urges us to growth and doing.

(Fire places a branch with "new" leaves on it)
Another bare branch may be used, with a few leaves attached. It is placed at the South of the Great Tree. The leaves can be cut from construction paper, or can be appropriated from any silk arrangement which has detachable leaves, if the season does not permit the use of actual leafing branches.

WATER: I offer a season of fullness of growth, a time for life and joy — as the rains of the year encourage the need to grow.
The season of Water begins with Summer Solstice, as the Sun moves into Cancer, the cardinal Water sign. For ourselves as well as the Earth, this is a time of greater activity and much growth. The Sun is brighter as our lives usually are during this season.

(Water places a branch covered with leaves at the West)
This branch is an expansion of the concepts at Fire, with still more leaves or growth evident.

AIR: I offer a season of change, a time to celebrate past growth and prepare for a time of inner silence — as the winds bring scents of both harvest and decay to our lives.
As the Sun moves into Libra, the cardinal Air sign of the zodiac, at Autumn Equinox, the season of Air begins. The Sun is cooling; patterns and schedules are changing, and we begin to put on a bit of weight in preparation for winter. There is a hint of the cold to come, and the leaves begin to change their colors and fall from the trees. Within the smells of burning leaves and the ripening apples is the fulfillment of the promise of spring, as well as the chill breath of the coming death of the year.

(Air places a branch to the East, which has scattered, colored leaves and fruit shapes.)
These can be cut from colored papers, borrowed from silk arrangements, or gathered during prior autumns to be used as needed.

If you wish to plan ahead, then gather autumn leaves of all colors during that season. Set up the ironing board, heat the iron, and press the brightly colored leaves between two sheets of waxed paper. (Find the heavier wax paper. Most forms available in grocery stores now are only lightly waxed for use in microwaves and will not work effectively. You will need the fully waxed paper for this process.) Gently but firmly edge the point of the iron between the points of the leaves, and be sure to press carefully around the edges. This seals the leaf away from the air and oxygen, which would continue the process of decay. When the pressed leaves have cooled thoroughly, trim the excess waxed paper around the edges of the leaves. This results in the color and shape of the leaf being retained. They can be stored flat for use whenever you need that color or symbolism. A gift box for ties is excellent for storing them. Another method is to melt a small amount of beeswax in a shallow pan. Dip each leaf and coat it with the melted wax. Allow to dry and cool; store in a cool place.

NOTE: If the use of "real" branches is too awkward, or if you do not have access to such materials, you might want to let your imagination run free. Substitute as needed for the elemental symbols. Cotton puffs at the North suggest the cold and snow of winter. A butterfly at Fire is certainly indicative of spring — in addition, the butterfly is a symbol of the soul, as is the element of Fire. A flourishing house-plant presents the same verdant, full-growth image of the summer season. Aromatic flowers serve nicely at Air.

HPS: Ah, yes, and its roots shall be able to reach deep within me, the Earth Mother, for nourishment and stability.

This is a reminder that not all things are visible, even though they may be necessary for life to be. The roots of a tree are not usually seen but are required to support and balance the tree. They also provide the nutrients from the soil for the growth of that tree. Here, the HPS speaks as the Mother Goddess.

(HPS unrolls "roots" attached to base of trunk.)

Remember when I told you earlier there was more to do with the trunk of the tree. . . ? I meant the roots. You will need a roll of inexpensive twine or small hemp roping. Cut into 4-5-foot lengths and attach to the base of the trunk. Be sure that you have as many pieces of the twine cut and attached as you will have people in the circle. The volume of the twine can be neatly piled at the edge of the trunk base.

At the proper moment, the HPS can either go around the circle and un-roll each "root" and trail it to each individual in the circle, or she can reach before her for her own and then motion to everyone to do the same. In this manner, everyone would have to reach for and establish his or her own "roots."

HP: Within that unity must also be the vision of the differences within us, so that the scope of existence is not limited. The branches shall reach to the skies, and I shall give them strength.

Here, again, is the recognition that we are all different, yet we work toward that same goal of returning to the single source from which we all come. Perhaps the encouragement to reach is also here, as if "the sky were the limit." The one law we have is, "An ye harm none, do as ye will."

(HP extends ribbons attached to various branches to reach to each participant.)

You will want several 4' – 5' lengths of inexpensive paper ribbon approximately one inch wide. Attach a small piece of paper to one end, marked with the name of the tree and its symbolism or meaning. Beginning with that end, roll it compactly and attach the other end to the branches. Space them evenly around the tree, making sure that there are as many attached as you will have participants in circle.

Mark them or place them so that the HPS unrolls the Willow, and the HP has the Oak.

At this point in the ritual, the HP unrolls each "branch" and hands the loose end with the paper to a participant. It might be simpler to prepare these "branches" and staple or attach them to the inside of the trunk top (if you use the posterboard tree), allowing them to hang loose inside the trunk. Then you would not have to roll or unroll the ribbons, and each one would be easy enough to pull out to extend to a circle member. However, this would need to be done to the inside of the trunk before the ritual begins, thus hiding the future "growth" of the tree.

HPS: I am the Weeping Willow. I express the ability of the Goddess to feel deeply and to weep — tears of joy or of sorrow.

The HPS reads from the description written on the paper attached to the tip of her "branch." The HP does the same with the ribbon designated for him.

HP: I am the Oak. The strength of the Sun God, the Sky Father, is seen in me.

Part. 1: I am the Maple. The inner sweetness of life, the union of the God and Goddess can be tasted in the sap I bring in the spring.

Part. 2: I am the Pecan. In my shade is the shelter found in the love of the Mother–Father. I provide food for the body as they give food for the soul.

Part. 3: I am the Pine. I am sacred to the God, and show His gentler side. I am ever green and growing — as is His compassion.

Part. 4: I am the Cedar — symbol of the Goddess. I am the pleasurable scent of purification, and protection from unpleasantries. I, too, am green throughout the year, just as the presence of the Goddess is always with you.

NOTE: Add other trees and meanings as necessary. It would certainly be easy enough to use the basic meanings of the Moon trees, if desired, and write a one-sentence statement of its God or Goddess characteristic. When all the trees have spoken, move on to the rest of the ritual. Linking hands at this point would be a further reinforcement of the concept of unity.

HP: Let us take a moment to examine our roots, the depths to which they reach, the movement of our branches in the skies, and how we each reflect the Great Tree in our growth.

MEDITATION TIME:
    Allow a few moments for each member of the circle to consider him- or herself and the qualities of the Great Tree Concept within them. Counting heartbeats is an excellent means. For a short moment of meditation, count to 39 heartbeats. For longer time frames, consider 60 or 99.

HPS: Remember the All that you are in your Thoughts, which are your branches piercing the skies.
(Air symbol is shared around the circle)
    A small bowl with cedar wood shavings or needles would be a good symbol for Air in this ritual, as it has an obvious scent which comes from a tree. Sandalwood is another good choice.

HP: In the expression of your energies is your growth, the reflection of the Great Tree which others see within you.
(Fire symbol is shared)
    A lively, healthy houseplant would serve well for this element in this rite, as the energies would be easily felt and seen.

HPS: Remember as your love flows that it is the life-force within you, the sap which expresses the sweetness of life.
(Water symbol is shared)
    Just plain water in the Chalice would be most appropriate, as a tree cannot grow without a source for that nourishment. A tree liqueur would also be suitable. I would suggest something like Cointreau (which has an orange flavor), Frangelico, or similar hazel-nut liqueur.

HP: In the dedication and surety of where you stand, remember from whence you came, and the source of your strength, and your roots to the past which enable your future.
(Earth symbol is shared)
    Regardless of what else I may have tried to share within this ritual, the soul-seed, the kernel of its meaning, can be summed up in these next three sets of words. Thus, I pass on to you the gift of the words given to me years ago by a dear friend. They are shared in the hopes that they will become a gift of love you would also wish to share with others.

HPS: May we grow, as the trees in the forest, each beautiful in our own way...

HP: Our roots reaching into the same rich earth ...

HPS: Our branches reaching to the same bright sky.
(HP gives each participant a seed)

If you take just a bit of thought and effort in the week or two before you conduct this ritual, you can make this segment most effective. As you cut an apple, orange, grapefruit, or any other fruit in preparation of your meals, save the seeds instead of discarding them. Thus, even the seeds you offer in the ritual are as different as each member of the circle is unique.

HP: May we each grow to our full beauty from the seed we now are.

No matter how long we have studied, how well we have mastered any number of skills, or however much we may be loved and respected by those around us, we are at any specific moment in time only as seed — just beginning to grow.

(Chant: The God, he is alive, Magic is afoot. The Goddess is a Tree — Her Magic is in Me!

This is an excellent chant — balanced and polarized — with which to charge the seeds the circle members have been given.

Most nurseries have fiber cups in which a seed can be planted to begin growth indoors. When the seedling is ready to be transplanted, the entire unit is placed in the ground, which prevents disturbance or trauma to the roots or the plant. Having small containers like these and a bowl of potting soil in the circle permits each participant to plant and water their seed within the circle as a symbol to take with them.

HPS: We are united in our strength and faith, yet we can delight in our differences which reflect the All in all.

THANKS TO THE DEITIES:

This is done in whatever form you prefer, or have found works best for you. Keep in mind that one does not command the deities. We invite them to share with us. We thank them for their presence and their participation. We lovingly release them to go as they will or stay as they choose. Courtesy with the deities is fully as important as courtesy with elders and people of authority in our own race. Besides being thoughtful and a measure of background and breeding, courtesy gets you further than rude demands!

DISMISSAL OF SPIRITS:

This may be accomplished in a very formal pattern of wording, or may be phrased as feels right to you at the time, as you would talk with friends. Each spirit or elemental force may be thanked individually, or in a combined farewell which speaks to all of them.

At larger gatherings you will frequently hear the dismissal of the spirits, which includes the option to go or to remain and share the experience a bit longer. "Merry Meet and Merry Part" is a phrase you will hear used often. With some groups, it is expanded to include: ". . . and Merry Meet again."

Because elementals are like small children with very short attention spans (and a tendency to be distracted from designated duties), the very formal dismissal works well (just as you have to remind the human youngster to finish putting up the dishes, take out the trash, or come straight home from school or a friend's house). Such a dismissal might be worded as follows:

"All Spirits brought forth by our actions here this night are hereby dismissed, with love, in accordance with our will and our purpose. Upon completion of your appointed tasks, return to your natural habitat — harming no one and nothing on your way. As we will . . . so mote it be."

This formal dismissal of the spirits draws upon ceremonial influences and is usually ended with what is called a sign of silence, a gesture used in many lodges which practice ceremonial magic. However, it works just as well without any stylized movements or posturing. If the esoteric traditions are of interest, I would suggest examining books which contain portions of the Golden Dawn materials and practices.

CIRCLE IS ENDED:

This may be done in conjunction with the dismissal of the spirits. Some circles dismiss one element at a time, extinguishing that quadrant guard as they bid farewell. As the circle is released, compass point by compass point, the retaining circle of sacred space is also negated and completely eliminated by the completion of the banishing circuit.

However you choose to close your magical circle, it must be closed or ended before you leave it. If the participants choose to have the circle "open, but not broken," there is freedom to go back and forth, visit, feast, or whatever, following the ritual. Doing this within the semi-confines of a partial circle is certainly all right. However, before too much wine has been consumed, or enough time passes so that everyone is in a hurry to get home, the circle must be completely grounded.

Much of our Craft has come from or been influenced by the witchcraft of the British Isles, where magical or mystical circles abound as geophysical fact. There are fewer known "Magical Places" here in our country. For that reason, many witches and pagans choose to end the circle by linking hands and lowering them to touch the Earth. As they do, they "see" that magical circle literally sinking into the very soil which forms the country in which we live, adding our magic to our land rather than being content with the fact that magical locations exist elsewhere in the world. The phrasing I have heard used in this context (in Oklahoma, Texas, New Jersey, Massachusetts, and California) is generally indicated below:

"This circle sinks into the Earth. It has never been and will ever be."

It is both a comforting and frightening feeling to know that whatever you do with your magic shall forever be a part of the very atoms of life which form the planet on which we live. That knowledge alone should make us extremely cautious as to the limits to which we take our magic and what results we desire in our working.

"Have I forgotten something?"

Before the Ritual Begins

The rituals in this book were written as a learning exercise and a teaching aid. Extra effort was made to combine all input and stimuli, with the goal of enhancing ritual experience, in order to learn the potential of the ceremony, and discover the more subtle influences related to that rite.

If you are using these rituals for personal meditation, many of these additions will be easily visualized, but are not required in physical form unless you choose to use them. On the other hand, if you are working with a group and wish to utilize any added support for the impact of the vocal portion of the rite, the following pages provide suggestions and shortcuts to creating those enhancements—or what some people would consider "stage dressing." Whatever you consider it, we'll be looking at how to create a mood or atmosphere which harmonizes with the particular Moon or solar celebration you have in mind.

One idea to be emphasized is that all items and support material are symbolic in form. Unfortunately, many of the sacred trees on which the rituals focus do not have easily identifiable North American counterparts. Thus, any reference to a specific "tree" related to the extra items used in the ritual is intended to be symbolic. Depending upon where you live and sources available to you, whatever item is actually used as that symbol may really be of any other wood rather than the "real one." If you have access to the genuine item—such as an oak, birch, or willow—wonderful. However, don't become so intent upon fact that you miss the force behind the symbolism in the ritual.

For example, suppose you want to include grapevines as decoration for a Vine Moon ritual and have no source for the actual vines. Simply utilize lengths of any twining growth which, by intent, become "Vine" insofar as your purpose is concerned. An alternative would be to use lengths of twine or hemp, which can be found at most hardware stores. Suppose the Moon in question is a Reed Moon and you can't get to a flower shop to pick up cattails. If all you can easily use happens to be wax-leaf legustrum, then use the legustrum and "call" it Reed. None of the directions and instructions are to be considered "iron-clad." They are intended as suggestions and ideas to spark your own creative thinking and make the force of the ritual more evident and available to you.

The more subtle nuances of any ritual are those facets which will later have the most marked result in the attitudes and lives of the participants. These qualities cannot be absorbed solely or completely at conscious level. They are deeper consciousness or "subliminal" factors which cannot really be taught—they must simply be understood and experienced within. There are a few things which are common to each of the rites, whether lunar or solar. Let's explore these first.

Each of the rites begins with a spoken passage which has no designation as to who speaks it. In each instance, these can be assigned to whomever the group leader wishes. I would suggest that the gender distinction be maintained, as an alternative polarity is part of the ritual.

Thus, if the first identified speaker is the High Priestess (HPS), then the opening or introduction should be spoken by a male. A woman's voice would be more effective for the initial comments if the first designation indicates the High Priest (HP). In most instances, the rites are written for the High Priestess or Maiden as first speaker in the lunar rites, and the High Priest or Guardian to vocalize the beginning of solar rites.

In each ritual there is a segment which can utilize a quill and ink or marker of some kind to draw the Ogham letter in the palm of each participant. This can be done with the fingertip, if desired, which will leave no visible mark. However, creating a non-visual character in the receptive hand, and making an actual mark in the expressive hand, is more effective.

Fairly similar phrasing in each ritual is spoken to the effect that the Goddess gives certain qualities to the tree in question, then gives the tree to her child/children (the participants). The symbol of that particular tree (the glyph or rune) is marked invisibly in the receiving hand at that point.

The participants are then reminded that it is their understanding of that tree within themselves which gives it form and expression that others can see. The visible mark is then placed in the palm of the other hand. These differences are part of the subtle support of the meaning in the ritual. Certainly, the rite can be celebrated with no physical motions or marking at all. However, there are three levels of impact to consider in shaping the lines of the appropriate Oghmic rune in the palm of the participant, which is to be seen by the inner eye of the participant only in the receptive hand, and visible to others in the palm of the sending or expressive hand.

First, the palm chakras are the nexus of a vast neural network (nadi), and are the easiest to open or establish in working order. Placing the glyphs in those locations, whether the participants know about or work with the palm chakras, has a great deal of impact.

Secondly, the difference between the unseen and the visible markings is important. The knowledge and the understanding of all that is behind or is represented by that glyph is within. What we hold within ourselves is something that is deeply and personally private. It is not subject to the view of others unless we wish to share it. What we express of that inner awareness and how we express it, however, is subject to the interaction of and with others. Thus, the second glyph is visible.

The third level is an extension of the second. The act of placing a "real" rune in the palm can deepen the inner response to the focus of the rite. When the rune is drawn in the receptive hand it should be drawn as if it were being written and read by the participant from his or her point of view. They are thus "reading" the gift given to them by the Goddess. The character marked in the transmitting hand is presented as read by another, just as the circle member's use and expression of the knowledge gained is seen and interpreted by those nearby. A common example of this concept is the practice of wearing a high school or university ring so that the emblem faces outward, for others to see and identify. After all, *you* know what it is and do not have to see it in order to know what it represents!

All of the previous discussion deals with the "why" of the marking, but let's consider the "how-to" aspect. Obviously, the easiest means of placing an invisible mark in the hand is to use the tip of a finger or some non-marking instrument. An actual quill with ink or food coloring appropriate to the ritual is certainly acceptable for the visible rune. For example, you might use a green ink or food color for an Earth Moon, blue for Water, red for Fire, and yellow for an Air Moon. You may choose to study and prepare an herbal ink appropriate to each particular rite. You may not have or be able to acquire an actual quill, but any pen, marker or fine paintbrush is suitable.

For deepest impact, a specific pen or marker should be used for that purpose only, and should be packed away with the other ritual equipment at the end of each rite. From a purely practical viewpoint, this assures that you have a marking instrument available in the circle should you happen to "forget" to include one in your preparations.

Another facet occurring in each ritual is the Feast of the Elements. This is somewhat unusual and is not common to all practices of Wicca. Most traditions use only the Cakes and Wine, representing the feminine elements rather than including the masculine Air and Fire. The use of all four elements in that symbolic union with life forces provides a balance of the elements, male and female. If I were to use only two in my personal working, they would generally be Fire and Water, as these would signify the Alchemical Marriage or Spiritual Union which is the flame of the Sun and the eternal womb-sea (thus the God and Goddess). They also symbolize the Spirit Fire (or Life Force) and Love. Keep in mind, however, that for some forms of practice, the Cakes and Wine do represent all four elements. The Cakes (Earth) are baked (Fire), and Wine (Water) has an aroma (Air).

The High Priest begins and ends the solar elemental feast. The lunar form is initiated by and closed by the High Priestess. The group leader who begins the Feast usually either drains the chalice or disposes of the balance as a libation. This is done by pouring the remainder onto the Earth or into a prepared container as a symbol of the Goddess receiving that gift.

By the tradition inherent in working with the trees, some of the Moons are more strongly dedicated to the Goddess. In those instances, utilizing the more "traditional" Cakes and Wine ceremony rather than the Feast of the Elements may be preferable. However, very little effort would be required to expand that portion of the rite to include the masculine elements as well. . . or to adapt the four-element celebration to only two, if desired.

According to the majority of the research sources I found, the vowel trees were not only sacred to the Goddess, but also were, by inference, female trees. Rather than thinking in terms of the Sun Goddess of Arinna, Oma-Terasu, or Grainne — all solar Creatrix — I chose to represent the Sun as masculine. The Sun, therefore, is the God to whom the Goddess gives birth, takes as a lover, sees destroyed, then births once more. Thus, the solar trees presented as gods are still sacred to the Goddess.

An addition to the rituals in the solar section that should be examined before the ritual is conducted is the addition of the Element of Spirit. The need for another voice and the symbol for that element should be considered before the ritual begins.

For our training circle, we chose to use various forms of Quartz crystals or points as the symbol for Spirit. If this choice is not "right" for you, then reassign the symbols as you feel is appropriate; or you may choose to eliminate that aspect of the Feast of the Elements.

At the beginning of each ritual is a section marked, "WORKING IS PLANNED." Whether you will be working solitary or in an active group circle, this segment does need to be planned in advance. In many instances, if you are responsible for leading the group, you may wish to simply designate a specific working to be done. Knowing the group and what is going on in the members' various lives makes the task much easier, as you simply focus on the type of working that is truly needed. You know whether the predominant needs relate to prosperity, centering and balance, inner strength to handle difficulties, or some other area.

However, several of the rites are more oriented to an individual working within the framework of the ritual. Prior to the rite, a brief discussion of the mood or force of that particular Moon and the type of working for which it is best suited can add a great deal of effectiveness to the results, whether for the individual or for the group working as a unit.

A circle works as a complete gestalt, but it is a good idea to always remember that the circle is composed of individuals. Thus, if you have a member who has respiratory problems, then you may want to limit the amount of incense used. If someone is reactive to a particular scent, then use an alternative scent which corresponds to your purpose.

The purpose of being a group leader is not to impose your will on others but to be aware of and responsive to those things which may interfere with or enhance the working or worship to be done. Nausea, hives, breathing problems, or even goose bumps have very little magical value.

One area which needs awareness and consideration is the use of alcohol. Enjoying a glass of good wine is fine, but the chalice in a circle is not just for one person or for those who like wine. A member in one training circle was quite allergic to alcohol. That created no problem; the chalice was filled with fruit juice or cool spring water! On other occasions, someone may be dealing with an ulcer or stomach problems. In such instances, just make certain that the liquid selected has as little acid content as possible.

The same approach works effectively when there are those in the circle who are recovering alcoholics. They have made a decision to take control of their own lives, and therefore deserve all the support we can give them as brothers and sisters. We are not offering them moral support when they must violate one commitment in order to honor another. They should not have to forsake the sharing of the Chalice because of its contents. Water is, after all, a perfectly acceptable symbol of the element of Water!

Not all the responsibility lies in the leader's hands, however. Many times, especially in open, public or regional celebrations, the High Priest or High Priestess has no way of knowing that a member of that circle is allergic to or is recovering from a habit of misusing alcohol.

Special people in various circles shared around the country have found ways to honor the Goddess and still share in the love symbolized by the Cup, even when it contained alcohol which they could not drink. In one instance, a young lady bent her head, and if she smelled wine as she started to drink, would kiss the side of the chalice reverently, lift it in a salute to the Lady, and pass it lovingly to the next person in the circle.

Another person, a recovering alcoholic, tipped the Chalice slightly, giving a portion back to the Earth, then brought the Chalice to the brow chakra as a salute of honor, or simply gently handed the Chalice on with a smile. There are many graceful ways to share the Cup within the circle without dishonoring personal commitments. Only twice have I witnessed someone refusing a Chalice which contained alcohol in a petulant manner — which detracted from the sharing experience for others in the circle.

Each tree-ritual chapter contains notations as to what will be needed, suggestions on making items indicated in the rite, and other helpful hints. If you plan to use these lunar ceremonies for a group, it would be a good idea to at least re-read those pages before time to begin.

If someone asked you to direct a play on a particular date, you would certainly read the script before the time for the opening curtain. Otherwise, how would you know how many characters you would need, what kind of props, when to dim the house lights, or even whether it was a musical, a comedy, or a tragedy?

Rituals present the same situation. Leading or directing any ritual is a matter of knowing ahead of time whether members of the circle need to speak for the elements or another persona, what candle color supports and harmonizes with the purpose of that rite, when a moment of silence is needed, and whether a chant would enhance or detract from the mood or impact.

So, read the ritual! Decide whether you want to make salmon balls for Earth at Hazel Moon or want to use goldfish-shaped soup crackers. Check to see whether the ritual calls for each of the elements to speak, then assign circle members (or ask for volunteers) to represent the quadrants and elements. If there is a place for an invocation and response to it, be sure to have the necessary information at hand. Also, make certain that whoever is invoking or responding to an invocation is not only capable but also prepared to fulfill that task properly.

Determine whether the true impact of the rite is best presented by having the group leaders speak the "extra" or "element" portions or by encouraging the active participation of the circle members. In many circles the High Priest and High Priestess handle any invocations or responses. Having some training or sense of responsibility in those areas is a necessity. However, those who serve as Maiden (assisting the High Priestess) or Guardian (aiding the High Priest) should be encouraged in the development of that same strength, confidence, and ability. After all, people in these positions are supposed to be able to step in and take over for the leaders when necessary. It would be a wonderful idea for them to know how to do so and have some degree of confidence (and experience) in performing such duties.

If you are the circle leader and have never heard of a particular God or Goddess, do yourself (and the group) a favor by spending a few moments with your mythology books and **looking them up!** If you don't understand the purpose and impact of what is being done or said, and you are in charge, then how can you expect the members of the circle to fully experience what is being shared? Even in a solitary working, a reasonable foundation of related knowledge prepares you for concepts presented in the ritual.

Read and/or write the ritual. Research the background and know that you understand the intent and purpose of the rite you plan to observe. Cleanse the physical self. Gather your tools, accessories, and ritual equipment. Ready yourself mentally, emotionally, and spiritually, then prepare the physical temple, including your own body. When all this is done, then you have it all together. Enter the circle with Perfect Love and Perfect Trust. Be centered and balanced, not only with the God and Goddess, but also with those who share the circle, as well as within yourself. Now that you are ready, the ritual may begin.

Invocations and Responses

Each person approaches invocations or oracles and the responses to them in his or her own way. Included here are a few brief descriptions of the ways in which various forms of training suggest that invocations be handled. Once again, try each of them and find which one is "you," whether you are calling the God or Goddess into evidence or you are the circle member responding to that spiritual call.

Invoking Techniques

All material presented in this chapter is based on the assumption that the individuals using these techniques will have already cast a sacred circle and will thus be invoking or being receptive to aspecting the God or Goddess while in a protected or sacred space. There are some strange or unfriendly astral entities floating around who would love to have an invitation to "crash the party," so to speak. If the Lord or Lady chooses to aspect within you in casual moments, that is one thing. However, as we are human priests and priestesses and not deific, it is in our best interests to be sure we are within a circle before we invite them into ourselves.

The first-and-foremost factor is to desire sincerely that the God or Goddess you are calling really be present in the circle. Center and balance yourself, then reach out with your heart before you utter a word of any invocative call.

If you are invoking the God or Goddess into another person you must establish a connection, rapport, eye contact, etc. with him or her. **See** them as the God or Goddess, and direct your invocative speech **to and through them**.

59

Unless you are using a "free-form" invocation, be certain that you thoroughly read the passage to be used before you use it. Be familiar with the words and phrasings, check on questionable pronunciations, and be able to offer the invocation smoothly. After all, it is a **formal** invitation to a deity to attend the circle. It is much more pleasant to respond to an invitation that presents your name properly.

Maintain that concentrated attention on the recipient of the invocation until he or she is ready to speak or give the planned response. Some calls are more powerful than others and have a greater effect upon the individual. Different people have varying degrees of receptivity to the force or energy with which a deity manifests. In addition, there is a significant difference in the impact or the manner in which various deities will present themselves. You need especially to be prepared to offer a steadying arm or hand as the reception is completed or released, as well as during the entire time the deity is actively present!

One common form of phrasing is found in many invocations. At the end of making the connection with the specific deity desired (the descriptive segment which identifies that God or Goddess), you may hear or use the phrase, ". . . descend into the body of this, thy Priestess (or Priest)." This is a beautiful form of invocation, but should not be lightly used, nor should it be the first method attempted. Both the person doing the invoking and the individual responding to that invocation should be experienced in its impact. Each should be proficient at invoking and sure of their own receptivity before utilizing this form.

Results

Don't be startled if there are times when the God or Goddess you have invoked decides that the "speech" you had prepared for them is not what they want to say and will opts for impromptu comments of their own. Listen carefully. They may even use the exact words which that particular brother or sister of the circle used before in discussing a matter. This can be disturbing, but truth is truth, even when it is uncomfortable to hear or when spoken in ordinary words and voices.

Response Procedures

It is vital for whoever is responding to the invocation to also reach for that presence. See the God or Goddess clearly in the eyes and form of the one who is calling a specific Goddess or God. Desire to come to that one whom you love and who is calling you to them. Reach outward for that total presence, but reach deep within yourself as well for awareness of it.

To be receptive to the energy of that presence, I was first taught to stand firmly with my arms crossed over my breasts, head slightly bowed, and to empty my mind of any extraneous thoughts. I was to simply be prepared to act for a brief time as a vessel or container for that deific personality or essence.

With that slight forward angle of my head, I would first notice the energy impact at the nape of my neck. This makes sense, as the throat chakra deals with communication, creative speech, and related areas. In Qabbalistic workings the throat also represents Daath, the sphere that is not a sphere, and the area of the Abyss. It would certainly be appropriate for those deities we invoke to come to us from beyond that Abyss. From that tingle or sense of an electrical charge at my neck, I could feel the energy flow through me, causing that strange little shiver or series of cold chills to ripple through my system until I could feel the extra density or energy throughout my body.

When I felt the presence was complete, I would take a deep breath, attune to it, and raise my head. For a space of about three smooth, deep breaths, I simply looked about the circle, making eye contact with each person there. Then I began the response. This was what I was trained to do when there was a specific response which was written into the ritual. Comments made by those observing when a full aspecting presence occurs with its own speech in mind indicate that it also takes that time to pause and identify before speaking. Isn't it strange! I guess our High Priestess knew what she was doing when she trained us! The drills she would put us through could be tiresome when we wanted to move faster and get on with really invoking or responding to the invocation. However, the first time I stood there feeling the changes and the energy flow and influx, knowing that something different really was happening, I was suddenly very grateful that she made sure we could handle the task properly!

Another method of preparing to accept that invoked presence is to stand in the Star or High Priestess position while the invocation is being made. This stance is just what the name implies. The recipient stands with a firm grounding, feet slightly apart, back straight and standing tall, with both arms reaching up and out. The body itself forms the pentagram points with the arms, head, and feet.

In this form, your "concentration" is on that deific force which you desire to manifest. Your body is the "lightning rod" that draws it to you. Here, the electric or energy tingle seems to simply flow down the arms and throughout the body. Once that energy is fully felt, slowly lower your arms to cross the breast as if enfolding that Presence within you, and slightly bow your head. When you are ready, then raise your head, look around you, and unfold your arms. Then you may begin your response.

In either form, I always had a sensation or image of the Goddess descending, aligning Her total self with my body (She always allows for the limitations of my lesser vessel), and then stepping into me as She surrounds

The Star Position

me. There is a strong sense of being enfolded with Her presence. I am safe, warm, protected, and very much loved!

One of my oldest circle sisters from my Mother Coven once described it beautifully. "It was as if the Winged Isis had descended to fold me safely and completely within her great wings while becoming part of my mind and speaking through me."

There are times when the recipient is not fully prepared and the invocation doesn't "take" or seem to be effective. There may be instances when a member of the circle might decide to use that opportunity to "grind their own axe," so to speak, and say things they feel need to be said. This will occur especially if they did not truly make the connection as a vessel for the deity.

Don't worry about it or attempt to be judgmental regarding what is spoken. Listen carefully. Even in such instances, there will be something of value shared. After all, the Gods use the body, brain, and speaking apparatus when they need to manifest. Why should they not use the thoughts and awareness of the individual as well, and speak to specific needs?

At the same time, the circle member who is giving the response must speak from the heart of the God or Goddess who has been invoked, not from his or her own viewpoint. You entered this circle in Perfect Love and Perfect Trust — or you certainly should have done so. To use this time and focus to put forth your own commentary or to redress personal difficulties with another circle member would be truly a breach of that deepest level of trust. Such an action would be a manipulation, not an expression of Love. The God or Goddess invoked may well let you (and the entire circle) know immediately that the words you spoke were not theirs. *That* is a lesson one does not forget!

Goddess Invocations

Earth, Divine Goddess, Mother Nature, who dost generate all things and bringest me forth ever anew. Thou art rightly named Great Mother of the Gods. Without Thee can nothing be born or made perfect. Thou art Mighty, Queen of the Gods.
(Variation of ancient Egyptian invocation)

Maiden, bring thy flowers;
Mother, bring thy child;
Ancient One, bring thy wisdom.

Bright Lady, Cerridwen, we welcome Thee to this circle in Herne's name for we are the blush of Thy Maiden cheek. We are the children you hold to Thy breast. We are the carriers of Thy ancient way. Bright Lady, Cerridwen, welcome!
(Invocation by Amber Moon Coven, Oklahoma City, OK
Shared at United Earth Assembly, 1985)

Invocation (and ritual) can be effectively done in rhyme. One reason for this is that rhymed verses are easier to remember than specific, unrhymed phrases. Some simple invocations to specific aspects of the Goddess could be:

Maiden Goddess, Purity and Light,
We ask your Presence in our circle this night.

Mother Goddess, Life and Fruitfulness,
We ask your Presence this circle to bless.

Ancient Crone, Wise One and Sage,
We seek your Wisdom to guide in this Age.

Experiment with your own creativity and write the verse or verses which call to precisely the form of the Goddess or God which you wish to reach and invoke. Consider the Lord of the Hunt, Laughing God, God of Life and Death, Mother of us All, or the Sun Goddess. Simply examine the qualities you wish to call to, and use rhyme to do so!

You will find another form of rhymed invocation in the Appendix on Songs and Chants (page 227). Whether it is spoken or sung, "Silver Lady, Golden Lord" will not only cast a circle, but also will invoke those deific presences in the circle thus established. Try it both ways, spoken or sung. Use only one verse and focus on the elemental influence you most need in your spiritual meditation. It is there to be used, and it works.

Presenting the Charge of the Goddess

These first two examples of the Charge of the Goddess are basic in form and are ones you might find, with slight variations of wording, in many books on the Craft. I was first required to learn them back in the sixties and have cherished them since.

The first paragraph is the invocation itself and is most effective when spoken by a male voice or by someone other than the person who is giving the Charge. The remaining segments are the response itself.

My personal feeling is that the response should never be simply read! I'm not saying that it has to be memorized (although that would, by far, be the most effective) or that you can't have the sheet of paper with the words in front of you, but that it **must be spoken as if it were being deeply felt and uttered by the Goddess Herself**. Let the words roll from your tongue: feel them, express them, and don't just say them; use any and all drama training that you might have ever had. After all, if the Goddess is speaking through us; doesn't She deserve our best?

If both charges are used in one ritual, it is an excellent idea to have two women read the charges. After all, while the Mother Goddess and the Star Goddess may be the same (and are, at ultimate levels), it does enhance the effect when the speaking voices differ in timbre, tone, and pitch. We don't often utilize both in one ritual, but when we do, two women represent the voice of the Goddess.

Charge of the Mother Goddess

Invocation:
Listen to the words of the Great Mother, who was of old called amongst men Artemis, Astarte, Dione, Melusine, Aphrodite, Cerridwen, Diana, Arianhod, Bride, Isis, and by many other names.

Response:

Whenever you have need of anything, once in the month, and better it be when the Moon is full, then shall ye assemble in some secret place and adore the Spirit of me, who am Queen of all the Witcheries. There shall ye assemble, who are fain to learn all sorceries who have not yet won my deepest secrets. To these shall I teach that which is as yet unknown.

And ye shall be free from all slavery. As a sign that ye be really free, ye shall be naked in your rites, and ye shall sing, feast, make music and love, all in my presence. For mine is the ecstasy of the Spirit, and mine is also joy on Earth. For my law is love unto all beings.

For mine is the secret that opens upon the door of youth. Mine is the cup of the Wine of Life and the Cauldron of Cerridwen, which is the Holy Grail of Immortality.

I am the Gracious Goddess who gives the gift of joy unto the heart of man upon Earth. I give the knowledge of the Spirit Eternal, and beyond death I give peace and freedom and reunion with those who have gone before.

Nor do I demand aught of sacrifice, for behold, I am the Mother of all things, and my love is poured out upon the Earth.

Charge of the Star Goddess

Invocation:

Hear ye the words of the Star Goddess. She in the dust of whose feet art the hosts of Heaven, and whose body encircleth the universe.

Response:

I am the beauty of the green Earth, and the white Moon amongst the stars, and the mystery of the Waters, and the desire of the heart of men. I call unto my soul to arise and come unto me. For I am the Soul of Nature who giveth life to the universe, from me all things proceed and unto me all things must return. Beloved of the Gods and men, whose innermost divine self shall be enfolded in the raptures of the Infinite, let my worship be in the heart. Rejoice, for behold, all acts of love and pleasure are My ritual; therefore, let there be beauty and strength, power and compassion, honor and humility, mirth and reverence within you. And thou who thinkest to seek me, know that all thy seeking and yearning shall avail thee naught unless thou knowest the Mystery: that if that which thou seekest thou findest not within thyself, thou wilt never find it without thee. For behold, I have been with thee from the beginning, and I am that which is attained at the end of desire.

You will find beautiful and highly effective invocations to the Moon Goddess, Pan, and others in several of Dion Fortune's books. I would certainly recommend that you read and utilize the material in *Sea Priestess, Moon Magic, Goat-foot God, The Winged Bull,* and her other writings. Another excellent source is the Fellowship of Isis, Huntington Castle, Clonegal, Enniscorthy, Eire. Direct your queries to Lady Olivia Robertson, and remember to include an international reply coupon instead of an SASE with American stamps.

There are so many facets and dimensions of the God, just as there are of the Goddess. It would be difficult to find one single invocation which could encompass that enormity, but I still feel that the first invocation I learned, of Golden Dawn workings, does just that.

> *Holy art Thou, Lord of the Universe!*
> *Holy art Thou whom Nature hath not formed!*
> *Holy art Thou, the Vast and Mighty One!*
> *Lord of the Light and of the Darkness!*

Invocation of the Horned God

Hunter, bring thy prowess. Warrior, bring thy skill. Father, bring thy guidance. Ancient One, Horned Crowned, we welcome Thee to this circle in Thy Lady's name. For we are the flight of the arrow from Thy bow. We are the edge of the sword in Thy honor. We are the spark of the flame of Thy love. Ancient One, Horned Crowned, welcome!
> (Invocation by Amber Moon Coven, Oklahoma City, OK
> Shared at United Earth Assembly, 1985)

Charge of the God

I am the fire within your heart . . . the yearning of your soul. I am the hunter of knowledge and the seeker of the holy quest.
I — who stand in the darkness of light am He whom you have called Death.
I — the consort and mate of Her we adore, call forth to thee. Heed my call beloved ones, come unto me and learn the secrets of death and peace.
I am the corn at harvest and the fruit on the trees.
I am He who leads you home.
Scourge and Flame, Blade and Blood — these are mine and gifts to thee.

Call unto me in the forest wild and on hilltop bare and seek me in the

Darkness Bright.

I—who have been called Pan – Herne – Osiris – and Hades, speak to thee in thy search. Come dance and sing; come love and smile, for behold: this is my worship.

You are my children and I am thy Father. On swift night wings it is I who lay you at the Mother's feet to be reborn and to return again.

Thou who thinks to seek me, know that I am the untamed wind, the fury of storm and passion in your soul. Seek with courage lest you be swept away in thy seeking.

Seek me with pride and humility, but seek me best with love and strength. For this is my path, and I love not the weak and fearful.

Hear my call on long winter nights and we shall stand together guarding Her Earth as She sleeps.

(Shared by Coven Phoenix — Odessa, Texas)

Wine Blessing as an Invocation

There will be times when Drawing Down the Luminaries will be the only form of invocation you wish to use. In those instances you may wish to utilize a form of the Wine Blessing we mentioned in an earlier chapter. The following is one form of both Wine Blessing and Drawing Down the Luminaries.

High Priestess and High Priest stand or kneel facing each other, she with the athame and he with the Chalice. They alternate the invocation and speak simultaneously for the last statement, which is made as the athame is lowered into the waiting Chalice. This is done in either a brisk, firm movement, or with a gentle reverence. It is never a casual motion as one would use in dunking a donut in your cocoa or coffee!

> **HPS:** *The Sun is born,*
> **HP:** *And the Earth awakens to its passion.*
> **HPS:** *The Sun shines through the heavens,*
> **HP:** *And the Waters are drawn to it,*
> **HPS:** *To fall again to Earth*
> **HP:** *And thus complete the cycle.*
> **BOTH:** *The Spear to the Cauldron,*
> *Spirit to Flesh,*
> *Man to Woman,*
> *Sun to Earth!*

Blessing is completed, and athame and Chalice are returned to the altar.

(Shared by Circle of the Unicorn, 1978)

This is a procedure which you will have to work with to determine your preference. In most covens, the High Priestess holds the chalice, the High Priest the blade. Reversing those patterns may raise a few eyebrows, but you owe it to yourself and your working to try it.

One hard-line Gardnerian High Priest compared the two forms. He later commented: "When I hold the *Athame,* the feeling is like penetration in making love. When I held the *Chalice* just now, it became more the Descent of the Goddess. There is a definite difference in feeling and response. It is a much higher vibration and is not bound to Earth images at all."

Become familiar with these invocations and responses. Begin collecting those you find of value and which touch a special chord of response within you. Take the time to write invocations for your specific ritual needs and keep them on file for later use and to share with others.

Even if you only use these or similar invocative passages in your own meditation, rather than writing your own, you will enhance your contact with the God and Goddess, and will strengthen your ability to establish and maintain that connection. May the Light of the God and Goddess be with you, and within you.

"Unto each tree is a Season . . ."

Rebirth — Silver Fir
Ritual Preparation

In keeping with the season, branches of evergreens may be used to form the circle. Evergreens and cones decorate the altar. The altar candles are white. In the center of the circle are the service candle and the marker for placing the Ogham letter in the hand.

Any pine, sandalwood, or woodsy scent is an excellent choice for incense for this ritual. Symbols of rebirth — such as the Phoenix — seeds, or an egg are suitable for circle decoration.

The High Priest will need a container holding small cones which have been dipped in wax. Either a cauldron or fireplace will be required in which to burn the cones.

Small sections of fir, pine, or spruce, with needles still attached at one point, will need to be placed within easy reach of the High Priestess.

For the four-fold feast, you will need one small evergreen branch at Air, one wax-dipped pine cone ready to light at Fire, a chalice with a lightly salty water solution at Water, sunflower seeds at Earth, and a clear quartz cluster or sphere to represent Spirit.

The easiest way to dip the cones is to melt leftover bits of wax in a little-used pot. When the wax is thoroughly melted, turn a small cone so that the point is downward. Hold the stem with kitchen tongs and immerse the cone in the hot wax, being careful not to put your fingers in touch with the hot wax. Lift each one out, allowing it to drip slightly, then place on a sheet of waxed paper until the wax hardens. Only a light coating is required.

You will want a clear quartz cluster or point that can be easily held in the hand to share for the symbol of Spirit.

71

The Season of Birth and Rebirth
The Silver Fir and the Palm

TEMPLE IS PREPARED:
CIRCLE IS CAST:
DEDICATION:
LUMINARIES ARE DRAWN:

The Phoenix stirs in the rustling fronds, and the Palm stretches its roots to the sea-womb of the Mother. The sweet fragrance of evergreen life-blood drifts upon the breeze and from the fires of the season. The breath is caught in anticipation as we celebrate new life with the Lotus Cup of Birth.

HP: *Rebirth approaches. We hear cries to Artemis, Ishtar, Ashtoreth, and She is there. Her protection enfolds the the new Sun just emerging from the womb of the dying year and holds it safe.*

HPS: *The light of the Mother glistens upon the new birth and the shackles of the yew fall away. In the strengthening flames of the Young Sun is the old year consumed.*

HP: *As Osiris and Attis I was imprisoned at my prime and bound to the old year.*

(Takes up small, used pine cones, giving one to each participant.)

The flames of my Lady's love burn away the deadwood which confined me. In that same way we each identify and cast away that which has marred our growth and would hinder our rebirth.

(HP lights his small cone from the altar candles and states the habit or attitude he seeks to eliminate from his life—procrastination, anger, etc.—and places his lighted cone in the cauldron or fireplace.)

(HPS begins chant: "Take the Old and Burn it" as members of the circle follow suit, lighting their cones and discarding old habits.)

HPS: *The metal of Birth is found in the name of the Silver Fir, which stands*

72

next to the Tree of Death, the Yew, whose metal is lead. Yet my silver is taken from ore mixed with lead, just as birth comes from death and death follows birth.

Thus do I give the Silver Fir the power of and protection over birth and rebirth even from the jaws of death. I give it boldness and faithfulness. Within it is good fortune when given to a friend. To the Silver Fir I give the time of Rebirth, the Winter Solstice.

To my Son, my Love, and to you — my Children, I give the power of the Silver Fir.

(HPS draws the birth vowel, Ailm, just beneath the base of the thumb on the receiving hand and closes the person's fingers over the mark.)

In your understanding of the cycles of life and the eternal Phoenix within you is the form and expression seen by the world.

(HPS draws the Ogham "A" in the expressive hand, leaving the fingers open as she finishes, and places a small sprig of an evergreen in the palm.)

Choose that quality or attitude of new birth which you wish to strengthen in your life as the rays of the sun grow in strength in the seasons ahead. From the ashes of the habits just discarded form the essence of your rebirth.

Chant: *The Wheel of Life turns slowly,*
   Slowly does it turn.
   Spring and Summer, Harvest Home
   And then the Sun's return.

HP: *Share with us the Feast of the Elements:*
   Share with us the wonder of that first breath of Life.

(Air symbol, a fragrant evergreen branch, is shared.)

Share with us the fiery strength of life's rebirth.

(Fire symbol, a blazing pine or other evergreen cone, is shared.)

Share with us the sea-womb from which we emerge and which stains our brow as we labor.

(Water symbol, a chalice with water very lightly seasoned with salt, is shared.)

Share with us the future of our Earth, reborn.

(Earth symbol, sunflower seeds, are shared.)

SPIRIT: *Share with me the Spirit of this Season.*

(Spirit symbol, a crystal, cluster, or sphere of clear quartz crystal, is shared.)

HP: *Look within yourself and see your own rebirth.*

(Pauses a moment for effect.)

> *Look also upon the faces you see around you, and share the new life there as well. The Wheel of the Year does indeed turn slowly, and our growth is not always as rapid or as smoothly as we wish. However, you have the strength of the Tree of Birth within you and can reach to give to your Brothers or Sisters of this circle, or to ask of their strength as you have need of their aid. Look deeply and rejoice in each rebirth, for it is your own.*

DISMISSAL OF THE SPIRITS:
THANKS TO THE DEITIES:
CIRCLE IS ENDED:

Season of Spring — Furze or Gorse Ritual Preparation

Altar candles are a light green. There are flowers and bright colors on the altar and scattered around the circle. If you wish to use a seasonal symbol for the center of the altar (used until the next turning point in the Wheel of the Year), you might use an egg-shaped votive holder for the symbol of the season of Fire. Many candle stores carry egg-shaped candles that will sit in an egg-shaped cup or stand alone.

For the Feast of the Elements you will need: two stalks of gold flowers (one which can be separated as individual flowers and one as a whole stalk), a candle in a small container so that it will absorb the heat from the candle, two small bowls which can be held one in each hand (one filled with wine), three fresh green beans (washed), the marker for the Ogham letter, and a point or cluster of green quartz.

Another touch in keeping with the season would be the use of the chenille or plushy "bees" utilized in floral arrangements for part of the Circle decoration. Small ceramic beehives, which resemble the old-fashioned round rope hives, can be obtained at many handicraft or variety stores. Some candle stores also carry items molded in that design.

Small plastic bags or cards would be useful, in or on which the sampling of seeds from four kinds of plants may be placed or taped.

For the four categories of growth used, consider the following suggestions, but let your final choice be those seeds which most strongly symbolize, to you, the purpose you desire to present.

Sustenance – Squash, carrots, radishes, or onions
Healing – Comfrey leaf, mint, peach, or feverfew
Beauty – Any flower seeds or chives
Purification – Sage, cedar, goldenseal, or hyssop

The Season of Spring
The Furze or Gorse

TEMPLE IS PREPARED:
CIRCLE IS CAST:
DEDICATION:
LUMINARIES ARE DRAWN:

The Cormorant's cry is heard over the waves and the fresh-turned earth adds its fragrance to the air. Emerging from a winter's rest, the honeybee flies to the hidden sweetness of a golden embrace.

HP: *I am the Lotus Cup of Initiation, the beginning. In my return to life, I blaze on every hillside and tame the winter sere. So, in your lives, you discard the lethargy of the winter Moons and begin to stretch and grow, marshalling your energies and purpose as a shepherd herds his sheep when they move to higher pastures.*

HPS: *Your minds feast upon new shoots of wisdom discovered beneath the mantle of the old year and its thoughts.*

HP: *From the death of the old year comes the promise of the new. You stand upon the threshold of the year as it returns to life, and you pace the furrowed fields, planting that which you hope to harvest in the fall.*

Plant well. Remember the need for sustenance and healing, but forget not to plant that which also provides for beauty and purity of being.

(HP gives each participant a small card or packet of seeds suited to the four purposes mentioned above. See preparation pages for suggestions.)

Call to the God and Goddess to guide your choice of plantings and its growth:

Chant: *On-niona, Jupiter, Ostara*

HPS: *As the life of the Earth awakens to the passion of our union in this season, I give the color of the Sun to the flowers of the Gorse. With the flames of the springtime Sun I give it freedom from the restraints of the old life. To the Gorse I give the Season of Spring and the time of the*

76

Vernal Equinox when day and night are equal and light begins to conquer the darkness.

To you, My Children, I give the Gorse.

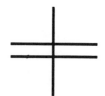

(HPS marks the Ogham "O" at the base of the forefinger in the receiving hand of each participant, closing the fingers over the mark.)

In your knowledge and understanding of the springtime flames of the Gorse within you is the blaze upon the hillsides of the everyday world that promotes new life and growth.

(HPS marks the Ogham "O" at the base of the forefinger in the expressive hand, leaving fingers open. She then places a single, small yellow flower in the palm.)

Chant: *Love Glow — Love Grow*
Making Love is making a connection;
Making a connection is making energy;
Making energy is making Magic;
Making Magic is Making Love. . . .*

MEDITATION:

HP: *Share with us the Feast of the Elements of Life.*

AIR: *Share with me the inspiration of returning life.*

(Air symbol, a stalk of fragrant yellow flowers, is shared.)

FIRE: *Share with me the growing light and warmth of this season's Sun.*

(Fire symbol, a candle in a warmed container, is shared.)

WATER: *Share with me the movement and change of this season.*

(Water symbol, two small bowl — one filled with water or wine — is shared.)

(NOTE: Guardian or first person in circle should be instructed prior to the rite to pour from one container to the other, then drink from the one newly filled before passing it on to the brother or sister next in the circle.)

EARTH: *Share with me the awakening life of the earth in this season.*

(Earth symbol, a long, fresh green bean, is shared. Each participant breaks off a portion to eat.)

---

*See Appendix D for complete words and music to this circle chant.

SPIRIT: *Share with me the Spirit of this Season.*

(Spirit symbol, a point or cluster of green quartz, is shared.)

DISMISSAL OF THE SPIRITS:
THANKS TO THE DEITIES:
CIRCLE IS ENDED:

Season of Summer — The Heather Ritual Preparation

Large, puffy blossoms of purple and/or white are perfectly suited to this seasonal rite. They symbolize the flowers of the heather and the linden. Scatter them and any amount of greenery about the circle, as this is the beginning of the season of full growth. Any fruits of the season can be used to add to that sense of fecundity and fruitfulness. Melons, corn, tomatoes, peaches, peppers, or okra and many other growths have reached maturity by this time.

A lovely addition to the circle decor for this seasonal rite is the potted heather plants that are so popular during the winter holiday season. If you didn't obtain or receive one at that time, you may be able to locate heather plants at your local nursery in the spring. They should be well-rooted and available for cuttings by the time you need them.

The symbolism of the bees and the hives carries over from spring, and continues to be appropriate to the season and suitable for circle decoration. The bees are usually mounted on small wires that can be twisted into arrangements or decorations. Scattering a few of these in and around the ritual area adds to the visual impact, especially if some of them are half-hidden near or under blossoms.

The center of the circle should contain a pile of stones set atop each other to form a cairn. Around it, place the heather branches and set the point or cluster of amethyst quartz as the capstone or top of the cairn.

Small golden-yellow colored stones are available in most lapidary shops. I have obtained small pieces of rough topaz for as little as thirty cents each, and occasionally better grades for no more than a dollar. It is best if these stones are at least partially clear, if not completely so, in order to best convey the symbolism.

Comb honey is usually available at grocery stores and some health food shops. Simply remove the comb from the container. Using a sharp knife, cut the comb into cubes or small pieces, placing them on the platen at Earth.

If commercial heather-ale is not available, you might wish to use mead, a honey-wine, as suitable to the season. Most wine and liquor stores will carry at least one brand of mead. If not, you may wish to make your own; however, that does require advance thinking (six weeks worth, in fact!). You might enjoy making it as a circle project, to use in all rituals once it has aged properly. You might also want to check the legal points in your locale related to producing alcoholic beverages. In general, I think that any household may make a specific, limited amount for individual or family use. This may vary from one state to another, but may be as much as two hundred gallons, far more than an average circle would need through the year. See the mead recipe given in Appendix D (page 223).

The Season of Summer
The Heather

TEMPLE IS PREPARED:
CIRCLE IS CAST:
DEDICATION:
LUMINARIES DRAWN:

The season's heat is upon us. The Queen of Heaven holds the Lotus Cup in Marriage and passion endures. The Heather blooms and the Asp-Queen seeks her beloved within its wood.

In the stillness the lion mutes its roar and lashes its tail. We hear the swarming bees and the song of the lark as it adores the Sun.

HP: *In the womb of the ancient hills is a triple cairn and the memory of an ageless giantess whose call of the hunt once echoed o'er the mountain slopes.*

HPS: *We pause at the center of the year, a balanced movement in the Dance of Life. Here is ripeness, fullness, maturity — the strength and union of the God and Goddess.*

Call to Them, and They shall come . . . .

CIRCLE: (Chants) Evoe Grainne, Ecco Lugh

HPS: *To the Heather and the Linden I give the honey-colored tears of its life-blood, the passions of love and battle, and the perfection of its flowers and their sweetness. It stands at the height of the summer Sun and is the Summer Solstice.*

To you, My Children, I give the Heather, the Linden, and the Cedar, each sacred to me. Drink of its tea and its ale; wear its white blossoms for protection, and accept the solitary beauty found in its purple blooms.

(HPS draws the Ogham "U" in the receiving hand, at the base of the middle finger, closing the fingers over the mark as she completes it.)

In your knowledge of Our Union within the Heather is the Beauty in the Dance, and the outer expression of your understanding of this season.

(HPS draws the Ogham "U" in the receiving hand, leaving the fingers open as she completes the rune, placing a small honey-colored teardrop or stone in the palm of the hand.)

HP: *Share with me the Feast of the Elements of Life.*

AIR: *Share with me the essence of the Heather.*

(Air symbol, a branch or cluster of heather, or other fragrant purple blooms, is shared.)

FIRE: *Share with me the strength of the Summer Sun, the symbol of the season.*

(Fire symbol, a tall, rosy gold candle, is shared.)

WATER: *Share with me the flow and ebb and rising tides of the Passions of Life.*

(Water symbol, representative of Heather blossom tea, is shared.)

EARTH: *Share with me the fruit of the Union of this Season. (Earth symbol, small cubes of comb honey, is shared.)*

SPIRIT: *Share with me the Spirit of this Season.*

(Spirit symbol, a piece or sphere of amethyst quartz is shared.)

DISMISSAL OF SPIRITS:
THANKS TO THE DEITIES:
CIRCLE IS ENDED:

The Season Of Autumn — The Poplar Ritual Preparation

Decoration for this rite should be as Autumn-like and Earth-toned as possible. Suggested colors for the altar candles are deep green and russet.

At each quadrant should be fruits of the harvest in the color for, or similar in nature to, the element they represent. For example, chili peppers of either red or green could belong at Fire, because of their spice and nature; but green ones could also be used at Earth because of their color.

If you collected autumn leaves during a prior fall season and sealed them in waxed paper, scatter them throughout the circle. If not, use fresh-fallen leaves of as many autumn colors as possible. This season is more colorful than summer or spring, but the shades are muted and of the Earth.

Shields for each participant can be easily made with either double-fold newspaper sheets or the similarly folded white tissue paper used to cushion gifts in their boxes. Maintain the original crease and fold in half again. Cut a wide triangle from that resulting multi-fold corner. When unfolded, it will provide an opening that slips easily over the head so that it hangs as a "shield." The hole can be cut nearer one end, but the bib effect is not as aesthetically pleasing as the short shield look.

The cauldron or brazier should contain well-lighted coals for the discarding of the shields, so that the thin paper shields will catch fire promptly and burn quickly. Otherwise, the laborious process of attempting to discard the shields will detract from the purpose and mood created. A service candle can speed the process if a shield only smoulders, rather than blazes, on the coals.

The High Priestess should take her shield, place it to burn, and take a moment to gaze directly at the flames it creates, while the High Priest comments about looking at yourself and your seeds. He then will follow her example while she talks of examining the harvest. This will set the pattern for each member of the circle to have a quiet time of introspection while his or her "shield" is burning.

Once the "shields" have burned, one of the circle leaders or a Maiden should unobtrusively place the ends of small dried twigs to rest at the edge of the coals. By the time the end of the ritual is reached and the charred "poplar twigs" are needed, they will be there. If they do not have a coal or a charred end, they will at least be warm and the desired effect will be created.

If you use the section of the ritual with the poplar leaves, these can be easily made of sheets of construction paper. Glue a green and a white sheet together, then cut poplar-shaped leaves from that composite sheet so that the underside of the leaf is white. Place a small safety pin near one end, or insert a hair or bobby pin for ease in "wearing" the leaf.

This rite marks the beginning of a time of dichotomies and contrasts. All around are the evidences of growth, yet the year is dying. Try to maintain this double-edged impact in the Feast of the Elements, as well.

For the symbol of Air, combine in one bowl a sweet, pleasant incense and a strong-smelling herb such as valerian. For Fire, combine a lighted votive in a container of ashes. Combine the two concepts at Water with pure water in a chalice which has been edged with salt, or by the use of two chalices, one of pleasing wine or water, and the other with salt water. Pass a platen or container of bright, fresh fruit nestled in dead leaves with little or no color to them.

Two pieces of citrine would work best for Spirit if you have or can obtain a specimen of the deep, brown-gold citrine, and have or can obtain another of the almost clear, bright-yellow shade.

At the end of the summer, shop in the school-supplies displays for a handful of the six-inch wooden rulers to use as the "measuring rods" given by the Goddess. While plastic rulers are sometimes less expensive, the added symbolism in the wood is more effective.

If you wish to use the gift of a bulb, I would suggest the iris bulb, as iris was the Goddess of the Rainbow, sent by the Mother Goddess to teach Her magic to her children on Earth. If the bulbs are properly planted shortly after Equinox, the resulting growth and blossom near the home of each circle member the following spring will continue the lessons and understandings of this season.

With many traditions, the rulership of the coven changes at this season from the Goddess in the form of the High Priestess to the God in the form of the High Priest. If you follow that tradition, the impact of that change can be thoroughly illustrated with carefully planned "stage movements."

As the High Priestess calls to the circle to listen to the words of the Horned Lord, the High Priest should move to a spot approximately one-third of the way around the circle from where she is. As he begins to speak, all eyes are on him; but none would be looking directly past him to see her. At that point, she quietly leaves the circle, reseals her exit, and slips away so that she is nearby but not fully in sight (just as the Goddess is not as visible during the winter months in the patterns of our Earth). In some circles, the Priestess places a circlet on the head of the Priest and removes her own to signify Her season of rest.

Autumn Equinox
The White Poplar, or Aspen

(September 21, 22, or 23rd)

TEMPLE IS PREPARED:
CIRCLE IS CAST:
DEDICATION:
LUMINARIES ARE DRAWN:

The Whistling Swan takes flight as the Season of Water ends. The rush of her wings stirs the bracken, and we see its reflection on her neck as she wings into the sky.

The seeds have been planted. They have been warmed by the Sun and by our energies, and watered by the rains and our desires. The tiny sprouts have taken root and grown. We have weeded around them, guarding and nurturing their growth. Now, Harvest Time has come, and we drink from the Lotus Cup of Rest from our Labors.

HPS: *The grains are gathered and winnowed. The vines grow heavier with their fruit. All that has grown is garnered and stored against need in the dying year, whether in our homes or in the dens and nests of the fields and forests.*

The Great Wheel turns once more, and with the season, we look upon our own harvest — within.

HP: *We attempt to spark the fires with which to light our search within ourselves, but the flames refuse to leap into being as we wish.*

Perhaps unwilling to really look upon our harvest, we find ourselves hiding behind shields of excuses and rationale.

HPS: *If we would truly see our harvest, we must remove the shields that have protected us in our battles through the seasons and clearly face our enemy — ourselves.*

We have been given the seer-ship of the Rowan, the magic of the Willow, and the wisdom of the Hazel. Now, it is time to use those gifts of Self from the Sidhe and to look beyond the shields we have falsely erected, not as protection, but as barriers behind which to hide.

(HPS removes the "shield" she wears, tearing it, and placing it in the cauldron to ignite. In beginning to burn, it will create the light desired. She continues to gaze intently at the flames as her shield burns.)

HP: *Look deeply, without flinching. You chose the seeds you planted. Did you nurture them? Were the choking weeds kept from them so that the seedlings were free to grow? Did you fail to water them with your desire and sincere wish for growth?*

Is your harvest what you sought when you planted in the Spring? Is it more than you expected — or deserve? Is the growth you garner less than you had wished? Do you find that what you planted is not what you desire when it has reached full growth?

(As the HPS speaks the following, the HP removes his shield and follows her example in burning it.)

HPS: *Seek within. Examine your harvest. This year of growth is known, but you, and you alone, must determine the value it holds.*

Seek within. Examine and know.

(Quiet time is allowed so that each member of the circle will have a moment of solitude to consider his or her inner self while their shield burns. When all have burned the "shields," the High Priest speaks again.)

HP: *The strength of the Sun is waning and you feel the coming chill. You stand upon the threshold of the old age of a dying year. The joys and regrets of your harvest fill you. Accept the sorrows and your part in their existence. Share with pride your accomplishments and achievements.*

HPS: *If you have honestly sought within, you have faced the giants of procrastination, neglect, rationalization, and laziness, and have triumphed over yourself. You know now what not to plant and how to care for the seeds which you will plant in tomorrow's Spring.*

Wear these symbols of that victory with pride for a Herculean feat accomplished.

(Maiden or HPS gives each member of the circle the "Poplar" leaf to wear.)

HP: *Share with me the Feast of the Season:*

Share with me the fragrance of the flowers of the Spring and the odor of decay found in wrongful harvest.

(Air symbol is shared around the circle.)

Share with me the memory of the Sun and the promise of its rebirth.

(Fire symbol is shared around the circle.)

Share with me the Eternal Sea: in rain and stream, river and lake, in dew and teardrop.

(Water symbol is shared around the circle.)

Share with me the bounty of the Earth at harvest, knowing that the bleakness of Winter will not touch you.

(Earth symbol is shared around the circle.)

Share with me this symbol of the Spirit of the Season, which is clarity of vision and knowledge of yourself.

(Spirit symbol, a sphere, cluster, or point of citrine quartz, is shared around the circle.)

HPS: *As Mother of the Earth, I give to you the black poplar, a funereal tree, but also the white poplar, a tree of resurrection.*

The Valley of the Styx I have filled with white poplars. Have no fears of that which the unknowing call a death, for I am not bound by the Earth and the petty weights and measures of Earth-bound life.

Mark your actions by My Measure, not that of the world which can only see the black poplar and the threshold of old age.

(Gives wooden "measuring rods" to each member of the circle)

I am a Shield to every head. Take my Shield for yourself, for those you love, and for all forms of injustice wherever they occur.

(Maiden marks the Ogham Eadha in the left palm of each member of the circle.)

I am the White Poplar. Be you also the Poplar.

(Maiden marks Ogham Eadha in the right palm of each member in the circle)

Be slow to the fires of anger as the Poplar is slow to flame.

(Maiden gives each member a charred "poplar" twig.)

Stand tall beside me, my children, and behold the resurrection of Life-in-Death and Death-in-Life.

(Maiden or HP gives each participant a seed or bulb.)

(HPS begins chant:)

> *The Wheel of Life turns slowly, slowly does it turn. Spring and Summer, Harvest Home, and then the Sun's Return . . .*

HPS: *You will not see me now as the bounteous Mother Earth, but as the Hag of Winter — the Crone. Know that I am here, but when you do not see me easily, or see your Father, the Sun, seek Him as the Lord of the Hunt and rest secure in our love and our shield for you.*

> *Hear your Father when he speaks — the Laughing God of Death and Life, Lord of the Harvest and the Hunt.*

HP: *Charge of the God.* (This charge is shared in the chapter on Invocations.)

DISMISSAL OF SPIRITS:
THANKS TO THE DEITIES:
CIRCLE IS ENDED:

The Season of Winter—The Yew Ritual Preparation

Gray and white candles on the altar set the mood for this season. It is a harsh, stark time of year. That imagery can be easily created by bounding the circle with bare branches. The sense of the season is further enhanced with fluffy bits of scattered cotton to suggest snow on the branches. The snow effect can also be created with a bit of water and Ivory Snow (flakes). Use medium speed on the mixer and whip the thick soap solution as you would whipping cream. It results in a soft, fluffy mass that really looks like snow.

If you should come across a fallen bird's nest during the year, place it in a lock-tight bag and save it for use in this ritual. Arrange one of the bare branches so that a portion of it rises into the air. Place the nest at an elevated fork and add just a touch of the cotton or soap "snow" to provide a visual impact of the lesser activity of the animal world at this time of year.

Unless you are Amerindian by heritage, it is illegal (and subject to steep fines or more) to have an eagle feather. You can be gifted with one by an Amerindian who feels you are worthy of it. However, the symbolic impact can be just as strong when you use a turkey feather. A wide variety of feathers can be obtained at most handicraft stores and some leather shops. Remember to use the smaller plumes for this celebration, as the bird for the yew and winter is the eaglet, not the eagle.

There are several easy ways to convey the tomb-and-rebirth concept visually. The simplest would be to use a wooden box or flat, oblong rock (like a tomb cover or horizontal monolith), placing a small sprig of evergreen in a Play-Doh base to stand on top of the "tomb."

If you have saved an oblong tin (like the ones some fruitcakes come in), place a small votive inside as the light of the god. Closing the lid or placing the cover on it will extinguish the flame. Then the evergreen sprig can be put in place as the "new growth."

This can be a depressing time of year for many people. Thus, a little extra effort expended in the symbolism of the Feast of the Elements is a spiritual tool to lighten that effect. Use your creative energies to develop striking, effective images.

A slab of bark can be sprayed or treated with bayberry oil to provide the symbol at Air. That seasonal fragrance is also evident in a "bouquet" of evergreen sprigs. You might tie them together with a bright red ribbon (to symbolize the dormant life energies or the blood of life-to-come) or add a small cone for decoration.

Use an empty one-pound coffee can with a votive as a shielded candleholder for Fire. Punch small holes around the can, beginning approximately two inches from the bottom. The holes will allow air to flow and provide tiny little "sparks" of light without permitting a direct glimpse of the flame. Once the lighted votive is placed inside, a loose cover of aluminum foil will form an opaque cap to enhance the imagery of minimal light. If no one you know drinks coffee, and you don't want to make a holder for yourself, check the discount import shops. They will frequently have brass votive holders which are cast in an open-work design that accomplishes the same purpose.

Pour a hearty, fruity, aromatic wine into a shallow cake pan or other container and allow it to freeze. Just before placing it in the circle, tap the edges with the handle of an everyday table knife so that it is irregular in shape. The baroque or uneven appearance of the ice (as you might see in moist hollows or stream edges) can also be created by pouring small amounts of wine in the container at intervals so that it freezes in an asymmetrical shape.

If you are one of those who never likes to throw away the flowers in an arrangement, use them to represent the resting Earth. A container of potting soil with a single dead leaf or with dried evergreen needles resting on the dirt will also convey the "death" and infertility of the Earth at this season.

A point or cluster of blue phantom quartz or light smoky quartz serves as the symbol of Spirit in the Feast of the Elements.

The effect of the winds can be created by placing a battery-operated tape recorder beneath some of the decorations or on the edge of the altar. Use a cassette of environmental sounds that features the winds. Once everyone has entered the circle, unobtrusively turn the recorder on and slowly increase the volume to an audible level. Allow it to play for a few moments and to continue while the High Priestess speaks; then slowly fade the sound out or turn down to a faint, background level for the remainder of the rite.

As winter is considered a season of "death," many groups do no working at this time. However, if you have no such restrictions in your practice, it is a thoroughly effective time to cast away old habits or patterns of living which have become "deadwood" in your personal life.

Whether you schedule a working or not, this season is one in which time should be allowed or set aside following the body of the ritual for individual meditation before the circle is closed.

The Season of Winter
The Yew

TEMPLE IS PREPARED:
WORKING IS PLANNED: This is a death tree rite. No working is usually done at this time.
CIRCLE IS CAST:
DEDICATION: Banba, Mercury, Hecate
LUMINARIES ARE DRAWN:

The wind shrieks through dark branches intertwined o'er the crumbling structure of stone. In the failing light the hard–drawn bow of the archer echoes the hiss of the wind. Beyond the wind and the arrow we hear the cry of the eaglet and the response of the she-goat to the bleating of her newborn kid.

A dying Sun casts its final rays to light the snow upon the cliff-ledge. Our vision fills with branches bare, darkening shadows, and the fading gleam of the reflecting snow. In the faint light we see the hand of the Goddess as She holds the lotus cup of Death.

HP: *Death surrounds us. We stand witness to the final moments of the Sun, the giver of life. The grains have fallen or been harvested, the Wheel of the Year turns and the living creatures of the Earth cannot be found in the somber scene.*

Lost in the howl of the winter winds is our whispered Spell of Knowledge. We cry to Banba to hear our voice.

HPS: *You stand at the deathbed of the Sun, He whom I gave life, suckled, and loved in his maturity. His light is hidden in the folds of my Earth and I become his tomb.*

From the grave of my Sun-Child-King comes the upraised branches of the Yew, with its foliage rich in growth in remembrance of his power and his strength.

To the Yew I give the last day of the year, the day of the Sun-King's final ray, and a lifetime which outlasts the glory of the Oak. I give to it the length of life taken from the Sun as the King's Wheel turns. Thrice shall the eaglet fly to build its nest in the whitened bones of its prey ere the Yew shall die with the Sun.

To you, My Children, I give the Yew. Within you, as you grasp the Yew, is the wisdom and the inspiration which is evergreen as the Wheel continues to turn.

(HPS places a small branch of evergreen at the base of the little finger and closes the fingers over it.)

Search the Yew within you for the hidden flames of the Sun which you must give to your world when its light fails and it despairs in the darkness.

(Marks an Ogham "Y" in the palm of the transmitting hand of each participant with gold ink, leaving the palm open when finished.)

HP: *Share with me the fragrance from the coffin of the vine.*

(Fragrant wine is poured on tree bark and shared around the circle.)

Share with me the warmth of the Sun-King's radiance that once urged the earth to life.

(Shielded flame symbol is shared around the circle.)

Share with me the chill of the frozen brook which once reflected the power of the Sun as it danced its way to the sea.

(An irregular slab of frozen wine is shared around the circle.)

Share with me the bleakness of the once-fertile earth as it rests.

(Container of soil is shared around the circle.)

HP: *Share with me the Spirit of the Season in which is the Shadow of the Sun-King's death and the promise of His returning Light.*

(Point, cluster, or sphere of blue phantom or light smoky quartz is shared around the Circle.)

WORKING:
MEDITATION TIME:
DISMISSAL OF SPIRITS:
THANKS TO DEITIES:
CIRCLE IS ENDED:

Day of Liberation — The Mistletoe Ritual Preparation

Colors for this rite should be green, gold, and white—the colors of the mistletoe. The most effective method is to form the circle with sprigs or branches of mistletoe. You can purchase fairly large rolls of the narrow, crinkly paper ribbon for very little cost at most variety or drug stores. This ribbon can be used to form the physical circle boundary on which the mistletoe sprigs are placed.

The central altar should hold three candles—one each of green, white, and gold—nestled in the mistletoe. A 6"- to 7"-diameter piece of flat styrofoam makes an excellent base into which the stems and candles can be inserted. This keeps the arrangement in order without extra candle holders or other accessory pieces.

Each participant is "bound" before entering the circle, but the explanation for the bindings is given within the circle. These "bindings" are around each ankle, wrist, and the neck.

The crinkly paper ribbon is ideal for this purpose. Cut lengths approximately two feet long. Hold the ribbon against the edge of a knife or opened scissor blade and pull the ribbon length firmly across it to the end. This will curl the paper ribbon inward. In this manner you can simply wrap the ribbon length around the ankle, wrist, or neck and it will cling without having to be tied in place.

This can be done by the Maiden or Guardian as each person prepares to enter the circle. However, it is more in keeping with the concept of the bindings if each person puts on their own. Before entering the circle, have participants place the curls of ribbon at neck, wrists, and ankles to simulate the five-fold bonds. The pre-ritual meditation time is ideal for this action.

You can produce completely different effects with the impact of this ritual depending upon the colors you choose for the bindings. Selecting colors that represent the elements as you see them would provide a pentagram of your body as the ribbons are put in place.

The order of mentioning the bindings will permit each member of the circle to visualize an invoking pentagram of Earth as the "bonds" are identified. In removing those same bindings, an Earth-banishing pentagram is created, which automatically invokes Spirit.

You will want to obtain a point, cluster, or sphere of black quartz to symbolize Spirit in the Feast of the Elements. If the darker form of this quartz is not available, utilize a larger piece of irregularly shaped Apache tear which has been well polished. The visual impact of sharp, stark edges in a reflective black will still be there, as well as the actual transparency of the crystal or stone on close examination. The "edge" will still be evident.

Since this ritual celebrates a "Day that is not a Day . . . and a Time that is not a Time," a sand-timer could be included in the circle decorations. Turn it to allow the sands to flow until each segment of the hourglass is half-full. Place it on its side within the ritual area, so that time does not "flow" during the ritual. This is a very subtle reinforcement of the concept of the rite.

The eagle is the bird assigned to the mistletoe. In this celebration you would use the larger feathers which were unsuitable for winter and the eaglet. Remember that the eagle feathers can only be held by Native Americans (i.e., American Indians), or by those to whom an Amerindian has presented one. Many leather or hobby stores will offer a variety of larger feathers which will serve as effective symbols for the plumes of our national bird. Our religious rituals do not require our spending time in jail.

Day of Liberation
The Extra Day of the Year

TEMPLE IS PREPARED:
CIRCLE IS CAST:
DEDICATION:
DRAWING DOWN THE LUMINARIES:

The golden sickle flashes in the changing light and the Lion-Eagle nests where the crag meets the sky.

You stand upon the Edge — On a Day that is not a Day,
                                A Time that is not a Time,
                                In a Place that is not a Place. . .

You stand bound in five-fold bond upon a Day of Liberation.

HP: *You are bound by the patterns of your thinking.*

(indicates binding about the head) (White)

    You are bound by the steps you have taken.

(indicates the bindings on the left ankle) (Green)

    You are bound by what you have done and given to others.

(indicates bindings on right wrist) (Blue)

    You are bound by what you have accepted from others.

(indicates bindings on left wrist) (Yellow)

    You are bound by where you are going.

(indicates bindings on right ankle) (Red)

(HPS takes up the mistletoe twigs and holds them as she speaks.)

HPS: *The tree that is not a tree sends forth new growth in the wintry chill when all else lies barren and dormant, cowering in the cold.*

97

For this strength and courage, I give to the mistletoe:

> *A Day that is not a Day,*
> *Time that is not Time,*
> *And a Place that is not a Place . . .*

> *To it I give Death and the power to Heal All.*
> *The ability to emasculate and to also bring forth life.*

> *To the Mistletoe, I give the Edge, that which is*
> *Between, neither rooted in the Earth nor living in*
> *the sky, and yet is both.*

HPS: *To you, My Children, on this Day that is not a Day, a Time that is not a Time, in a Place that is not a Place, I give the Mistletoe.*

(HPS gives each circle member a sprig of mistletoe and Maiden marks the invisible Ogham II in the receiving palm of each participant)

HP: *You now hold the Edge within and upon the Edge where you stand. Because it is what it is not and is not what it is, its form and expression are not for the world to see. It is within you. You are the Edge, the Gryphon-Eagle of neither Earth nor Sky.*

HPS: *Be ye wise in becoming an Edge of Magic. Lower your dreams into the Well of Wyrd beneath the branches of the Mistletoe, but bring their fruition carefully from its depths lest you stumble, spill its icy fire and are consumed.*

HP: *You may become the Edge, but the light shifts and footing may be uncertain unless you walk the Edge with clear Vision of that Edge within yourself. Be ye certain of the Edge which you may become. Seek, experience, and know Yourself.*

(Meditation time is allowed for each participant to consider him- or herself.)

HP: *Let us free ourselves from our restrictive bonds upon the turning Sun-Wheel. We call upon the Elements, Wise Ones, and the Gods of this Day to aid us in our efforts.*

EARTH: *I, Aeneas, have learned from my Father. While I may use the knowledge thus gained, I am not bound to it only.*

(Removes the green binding on the left ankle.)

SPIRIT: *I, Hercules, have accomplished great things, but I cannot rest upon my laurels. There are other tasks which I must do.*

(Removes the white binding around the head.)

FIRE: *I, Shu, know the eternal ebbs and flows of Light, and now must put to use my knowledge.*

(Removes the red binding on the right ankle)

WATER: *I, Osiris, cannot do all things alone; with the Magic of my Lady, we create life anew where none could exist before.*

(Removes the yellow binding on left wrist.)

AIR: *I, Balder, was felled because one young plant was considered to be less than it was. All things must be allowed to be all that they are.*

(Removes the blue binding from the right wrist.)

(HP and HPS use the "bindings" as a tie for the sprig of mistletoe. The circle follows suit.)

HP/S: *Share with us on this Day which is not a Day.*

HPS: *Share with us the view from the Gryphon's nest and its sweet fragrance of untapped potential.*

(Air symbol is shared.)

HP: *Share with us the changing light of the Edge, the Dawn and Dusk of what may become.*

(Fire symbol is shared.)

HPS: *Share with us the wells and seashores of that which emotion has yet to create.*

(Water symbol is shared)

HP: *Share with us the low yet lofty growth, the Edge of being Earth and Sky in One.*

(Earth symbol is shared.)

HP/S: *Share with us the Spirit of that which is Between.*

(Spirit symbol, a point, cluster, or sphere of black quartz is shared.)

MAID: *The golden sickle flashes in the changing light and the or Eagle-gryphon nests where the crag meets the sky.*

HPS: *You stand upon the Edge on a Day that is not a day, a Time that is not time, in a Place which is not a place.*

HP: *You cannot walk your Inner Edge if you wear the bindings or the Sun-Wheel or seek without.*

GRD: *If you find not the Edge within yourself, it will forever elude you in the Changing Light. Be ye sure of the Edge you are.*

WORKING:

THANKS TO THE DEITIES:

DISMISSAL OF SPIRITS:

CIRCLE IS ENDED:

"There shall be a Year of Moons . . ."

First Moon: Birch

CIRCLE DECORATIONS: One black and one white candle are suggested for the altar, which is covered with white. If it is possible, decorate the circle with barely leafing branches. Placed in the center is the "Death" figure from the Elder Moon. A cluster of shorter branches lie by the altar on the north side, a second cluster of similarly sturdy stems to the south. Near the altar are skeins of red, blue, and white embroidery thread and a knife or pair of scissors. Following the invocation and drawing down of the Moon, the High Priestess (HPS) turns and speaks.

INVOCATION: If you use the verses of *Hertha* by John Swinbourne, I suggest that you memorize them before the ritual, so that the impact of the verses is not lessened by the presence of sheaves of paper. In addition, the force of the eye contact possible made with each member of the circle during this spoken passage is immeasurably greater if you do not have to read the words. The voice then becomes the Goddess, not "just" a priestess's.

THE BESOMS (brooms): These can be made in miniature, approximately 7-8 inches for the "birch twigs," to create a finished length of 12 inches, or made more nearly approximating actual size by selecting 18-inch twigs and a 24-inch length of "ash." Remember, any wood can be used to symbolize the birch or ash.

ASH STAFFS: If you live where there is little or no access to trimmable branches for this purpose, dowel rods or similar sticks can be used. These are available quite inexpensively at most lumberyards and hardware stores, as well as at many variety stores.

WILLOW OR OSIER BINDINGS: These can be of any type of string or yarn. I'd suggest embroidery or crochet thread, which are usually all-natural in content, normally available in primary colors, and do not have the tendency to stretch as yarn does. In addition, they are less expensive to purchase and easier to use.

It is easier to trim away excess length when you have completed the besom than it is to add a few extra inches of thread or yard in order to finish your working. Whether you are working with the miniature besom or those more nearly full-size, you can allow adequate binding material by cutting 2- to 3-foot lengths of each color to be used.

Whether you use crochet or embroidery thread, yarn, or ribbon, select a basic white and the rich, pure primary colors of red and blue. The white strand is the Maiden's purity, red is the Mother's color, and blue is the wisdom and depth of the Crone. If your personal symbolism sees the Crone as black rather than blue, then your bindings will be white, red, and black.

MARKING THE RUNE: The first Moon/month is an earthy Moon. If you use a dab of food coloring to draw the Ogham character, select green for this ritual to symbolize the Earth.

PLEDGE: This practice began, for me, many years ago, when I had a constant difficulty in keeping my New Year's resolutions. So, I made it a new requirement that I could not claim as a resolution anything which I had not been doing or attempting to do for at least three days prior to the end of the old year. That way, the "new" resolve was continuing something I wanted to do, not starting something that "should" be done. Then it was a "gift" to myself.

You may want to discuss this idea before the ritual with the members of your circle or give yourself time for serious thought in a solitary meditation ritual. Although the ritual phrases suggest something pleasurable for yourself, it has been my practice to make that pledge or gift something which will become a gift of knowledge or heightened skill and ability related to my Craft. The rituals in this book, for example, were a result of that intended gift to myself one year. Another year at Birch Moon, I chose to carefully copy all rituals I had written or been given over a period of years into a special book. As you can imagine, those gifts to myself have continued to be something "nice for myself" for many years afterward, and in the process have strengthened my personal knowledge and awareness.

Birch
Moon of Inception

TEMPLE IS PREPARED:

WORKING IS PLANNED: In this Moon, the decisions are made as to what spiritual seeds you will plant in this year which is just beginning. Magical work in this Moon adds strength and momentum to those choices.

CAULDRON: nettle leaves, star anise, black malva flowers

CIRCLE IS CAST: (You may wish to leave the circle unlighted in the beginning. Hearing a voice speaking the first three verses of *Hertha* as a voice in the darkness or void can be very effective. If this atmosphere is chosen, have four members of circle prepared to light the quadrant guards simultaneously when the HPS speaks of clearing hearts and minds.)

DEDICATION: Choose deities of births and beginnings, those who created from limited materials or nothing.

> *I am that which began, out of me the years roll.*
> *Out of me, God and Man — they are equal and whole.*
> *God changes, and Man, and the form of them bodily,*
> *I am the Soul.*
>
> *Before ever land was, before ever the sea,*
> *Or the soft hair of the grass or fair limbs of the tree*
> *Or the flesh-colored fruit of my branches I was,*
> *And thy soul was in Me.*
>
> *First life on my sources first drifted and swam.*
> *Out of Me are the forces that save it — or damn.*
> *Out of me — Man and Woman, Wild Beast and Bird.*
> *Before God was, I AM.*
> (Excerpted from *Hertha* by John Swinbourne)

HP: *This is a time of beginnings, yet we still feel sluggish from the season of death and winter. Not yet do we really feel the increasing warmth and light of the Sun.*

105

HPS: *This past year has been fraught with hardships for each of us. Let us clear our hearts and minds of the spirits of that year to make way for a new year and new growth.*

(HPS takes up cluster of "birch" branches, striking the ground or the altar with each symbol of the year past, finally striking and toppling the death figure in the center with the Moon name "Elder.")

HP: *The old year is measured by its Sabbats.*

Circle: (In unison) *"Ailm, Onn, Ura, Eadha, Idho."*

HP: *The old year is marked by its Festivals.*

Circle: *Candlemas, Beltane, Lammas, Samhain.*

HP: *The old year is bounded by its Moons:*

CIR: *Birch, Rowan, Ash, Alder, Willow, Hawthorn, Oak, Holly, Hazel, Vine, Ivy, Reed, Elder.*

HP: *Death is destroyed and rebirth takes form.*

HPS: *No more the season of death. It is the season of life and beginnings.*

HP: *The Goddess leaves with us a symbol of beginnings in the Birch tree.*

HPS: *To the Birch She gives the first Moon of the year, beginnings, nobility, the tip of the thumb, Sunday, the driving out of evil spirits, the rod of office to one of thirteen, the Sun, a place in the hats of dead sons, and the resting place of Elija at Mount Horeb.*

HP: *To us, Her Children, She gives the Birch.*

HPS: *She places within us the knowledge of victory over death.*

(HPS marks the receptive Ogham letter "B" in the receiving palm of each person so the letter read from their viewpoint.)

Our words and actions give that knowledge form and expression to be known by others.

(HPS marks the expressive Ogham letter "B" in the transmitting palm of each participant so that it can be read by someone facing them.)

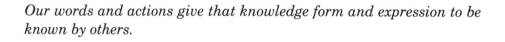

(HPS takes up Birch twigs, giving one to each covener as follows:)

HPS: *I am the Maiden: I am victory over death, I am beginnings.*

(Gives one branch to each.)

I am the Mother: I am birth, I am continuation of beginnings.

(Gives a second branch.)

I am the Crone: I am the guide to Rebirth, I am completion of beginnings past and the vision of those to come.

(Gives a third branch.)

(HP gathers the remaining "Birch" branches.)

HP: *Sacred also to me, as Horus, are birth and beginnings.*

(Gives one branch.)

As Osiris, victory over death and the path to rebirth is mine.

(Gives a second branch to each participant.)

(Each covener now has five "Birch" branches.)

HP: *To the future hidden in beginnings, we add the protection of the Ash.*

(Gives the sticks at the south of the altar to coveners.)

HPS: *And the Magic of the Willow, to build into this year shelter, clothing, food, and love.*

(Gives a long strand of the three threads to each participant.)

(HP/HPS take up the "Ash" stick and one "Birch" twig or branch. circle follows suit. They begin binding a besom, one twig or branch at a time. The chant is: "Flags, Flax, Fodder, Frig." It is continued until the besoms are completed and tied off.)

(Note: If one twig is bound with each chant, and there are four bindings with all twigs together, the total will equal nine, a number sacred to the Moon.)

(Besoms are consecrated in a joined circle. Chant: "Ashima, Ninimb, Anatha, Ra." Pronounced: *Ash ih muh, Nih nim, Uh nath uh, Rah*)

(With besoms still in hand, this chant lends itself to a circle dance, if desired.)

HPS: *In Moons and festivals just past, we have pledged our efforts and energies to removing deadwood, to balancing karma, but now, a particular action or series of actions for ourselves, as a gift to ourselves, is needed for this coming year.*

This is not that which is "needful," nor is it that which "should be done," but rather that which is born with desire and not from a lack or need. In this pledge, we do something "nice for ourselves" as a beginnings–gift from the Goddess to set a pattern of joy for the year ahead and in that joy, serve Her.

HP: *The Birch Moon of beginnings is here. We worship in its light. We are the elements of which life is made, and we share in the Feast of the Elements always remembering that any meal is a sacrament. Our brothers and sisters of the fields and forest have sacrificed their lives that the purpose of our lives may be fulfilled.*

(Maiden gives appropriate element symbol to the HPS as needed. HPS offers it to the HP, saying: "Share with me this symbol of the element of _____." It is passed around the circle, ending with the HPS taking a portion.)

WORKING: (This Moon should be one to draw to each covener as much of the energies raised as they need through the first Moon, rather than necessarily working for the needs of others.)

DISMISSAL OF SPIRITS:
THANKS TO DEITIES
CIRCLE IS ENDED:

Second Moon: Rowan

WATTLES OF KNOWLEDGE: Wood chips, or an inexpensive bag of cedar chips, can be scattered in or placed around the circle in this Moon rite, to symbolize the growths of the Rowan tree, which contains all knowledge.

ROWAN RODS: Three "Rowan rods" per participant need to be placed in the circle. These can be cut from branches with greenery at this time of year. However, for most of us, the climate doesn't cooperate. I substitute short lengths of dowel rods stained brown, to which I attach three silk leaves at the tips. Dowel rods usually are available in 36-inch lengths at lumber yards, some hardware stores, and variety stores. As I do not have woodworking tools, I simply have the lumber yard cut the dowels into three different lengths; then I sand the edges at home. There is no specific length to use. I choose 6-, 12-, and 18-inch lengths, because these divide evenly into 36"; and each can be divided by three. This also gave me three sizes for each set of rods, which made the subtle suggestion that each oracular gift may differ from another and that we each work in different ways with our gifts.

ELEMENTS: This Moon is ideal for having members of the group speak for the elements in the four-fold Feast. The "speech" of the element can be written on a 3 x 5 card for ease of use and convenience. In some groups, a copy of the ritual is provided so that each member of the circle may add it to their own Book of Shadows.

CHALICE: This is an excellent Moon for using cranberry juice in the chalice as a support or enhancement of the cranberries at Earth.

FEAST OF THE ELEMENTS: During the holiday season each year, I place approximately half a cup of fresh cranberries in a small plastic bag in the freezer to be saved for use in this Moon. The cranberries are tart and certainly attract your awareness by their taste, just as oracular input does. Their color, as well, is symbolic of the shade of Rowan berries.

Rowan
Moon of Vision

TEMPLE IS PREPARED:
WORKING IS PLANNED:
CAULDRON: Irish oak moss, eucalyptus leaves, uva ursi leaves
CIRCLE IS CAST:
DEDICATED TO: Eleu, Diarmuid, Iris

The increasing warmth of the Sun melts the drifts of snow on the mountain slopes and brings the rains of the season.

The Earth quickens; its first faint stirrings disturb the lethargy to which you have become accustomed. You feel the beginnings of your need to grow, a just-awakened realization of your own rebirth at the Winter Solstice.

You still sleep and dream, not yet ready to set your energies to growth.

As you dream, you approach a wood which is veiled in mist. Not clearly seen, it is a view which draws you, but not against your will. The sounds from the forest are muted, but you hear the calls of nearby ducks on rain-made ponds which swell across the meadows.

HP: *The skies lower and the grey-laden clouds open to spill their burdens upon you and your pathway. The lightning flashes, but not near the misted forest, despite the towering trees that draw its flash.*

You hasten your steps and enter the forest, for it offers some shelter from the downpour. Strangely, within the woods, the mist is lessened. You see a clear path which leads you onward. As you follow it, you feel a growing awareness of great import to come. A hint of breeze stirs the trees, and you almost hear a message in the soughing branches.

HPS: (Whispers slowly, barely audible, in sets of threes):

WITCH! WITCH! WITCH!
WITCH! WITCH! WITCH!
WITCH! WITCII! WITCH!

HP: *With the still sighing forest about you, you round a curve to enter a circle of stones. You have found your way through the grey mist, have passed the lightning bolts unscathed. A fragment of memory stirs within and you know that you have taken shelter in an oracular Rowan grove.*

Standing at the center of the stone circle, you find an enormous carving of a time-worn face, so skillfully created that life could be contained within it. Drawn to it, you trace the curves and lines and hollows of the visage with the tip of your forefinger. The great shelf of a jaw moves slowly to open before you. With wonder you see three rods of Rowan wood rooted within.

HPS: *You cry: "What would you have me do?"*

And the Oracle replies, "I am a wide flood upon the plain. Take you these, for within the wattles of knowledge you will find understanding of the flood."

(HPS holds a set of three rods in turn to each participant as she speaks the following. Each person pulls them gently from her grasp.)

You tug gently at the living rods, and they come freely to your grasp. You wait, but the oracle is silent and the great visage is still.

Turning, you retrace your steps, leaving the oracular grove and wandering once more on the misted plain. You feel a weight in your hands. Awakening from your dream to the quickening year, you find a circle of stones surrounding you. Held lightly in your grasp are three Rowan rods.

Studying the faces in that circle, you find in each one are traces of that visage in the woods. You reach to grasp the hands near you, knowing that they, too, are part of that wide flood and that they also seek to understand.

("Rowan rods" are consecrated in a joined circle for future use. The chant is: "Ileu, Iris, Shu.")

HP: *And the Goddess says: "I have given to the Rowan — the second Moon of my year — divination, oracular knowledge, protection against lightning and charms. I have given it the Quickening of the Year, the names of 'Witch' and 'Flame,' as well as all kinds of knowledge and science, and the knowledge of My sacred name. To its berries I give the sustenance of nine meals, the power to heal the wounded, and to add a year to the lifespan."*

HPS: *To you, Her Children, she gives the knowledge of the Rowan Tree Within.*

(She touches the tip of the forefinger to the center of the left palm of each participant, then closes the fingers over it.)

> *It will be your words and your actions which give that knowledge form and expression for the world to see.*

(HPS writes Ogham L in palm of right hand, leaving palm open when finished.)

HP: *The Quickening Moon is here, and we worship in its fullness, knowing that we are each the elements of which life is made. Share with us the feast of the elements of life. Never forget that each meal is a sacrament to us, as our brothers and sisters of the fields and forests have given of their lives to sustain our own.*

(Maiden gives HPS incense or early flower, symbol of Air. HPS takes it and turns to offer it to the HP.)

AIR: *Share with us this symbol of the element of Air, remembering the fragrance of the Rowan grove, the cries of the ducks, and the sounds of the forest.*

(Maiden gives each element symbol to the HPS as needed. HPS turns to share that symbol with the HP.)

FIRE: *Share with us this symbol of the element of Fire, remembering the brilliance of the lightning flash and the quickening warmth of the Sun.*

(Fire element is shared around the circle.)

WATER: *Share with us this symbol of the element of Water, remembering the mists which conceal that which we seek and the wide flood of which we are a part.*

(Water element is shared around the circle.)

EARTH: *Share with us this symbol of the element of Earth, remembering the knowledge of the forest and its recognition of all that we are.*

(Earth element is shared around the circle.)

(Feast is finished. The element symbols are returned to their quadrants.)

WORKING:
DISMISSAL OF SPIRITS:
THANKS TO DEITIES:
CIRCLE IS ENDED:

Third Moon: Ash

The only "extra" added to this Moon is the use of wood chips or slivers of wood symbolizing the vessels traversing the flood waters. These can be chips, if you happen to live where wood is chopped or woodcraft work is done with a plane. If so, then utilize the wedges or curls of wood that result from either task.

If, however, these are not available for you, then use your creativity and develop your own coracles. They can be made from construction paper folded and pasted to form the proper boat shape. Pipe-stem cleaners can be inserted as a mast, and triangular "sails" cut from other construction paper or cloth fragments. Wood-grain patterns are available in inexpensive, self-adhesive, vinyl shelf-covering paper at most grocery, variety, or hardware stores. Less than half a yard will nicely cover a smooth piece of cardboard, and boat or raft shapes can be cut from that larger piece and glued or taped together.

Toothpicks and glue will easily form barge or raft-type vessels. Spread a piece of waxed paper to work on. Simply dump a few toothpicks out for easy access; pull one through a small pool of glue, place another with it, and continue placing them next to each other until the desired size is reached. Allow to dry, and *voila!* you have a semi-instant coracle.

If you or a neighbor have a nut tree in the yard, carefully collect the outer half-hulls which encased the nuts but fall from them at harvest time. Most of them will split into four peel-like segments, but some will cling together to form a rounded shape. Dry the half-hulls naturally on the window sill, and store for this Moon the following year. You will have natural, water-resistant miniature boats at your disposal.

You may put as much or as little effort into these symbols as you wish. However, I would suggest making them as simple as possible, as the symbol they convey is an inner vehicle, not a speedboat. A plain, somewhat rowboat-shaped, flat piece cut from cardboard is adequate and forces the participant to look inward rather than seeing only the outer shape.

Because of the intense emotional content and impact of this Moon, using water in the Chalice is ideal. After all, if water cannot symbolize the element of Water, I don't know what could!

Ash
Moon of Floods

TEMPLE IS PREPARED:
WORKING IS PLANNED:
CAULDRON: ash leaves, broom flower tops, spearmint leaves
CIRCLE IS CAST:
DEDICATION: Tefnert and Ileu

Night still reigns and the waters of rebirth rise.

The spreading roots and branches of three mighty trees are gone. The ground where they once stood thickens with new growth.

Yet the spirit of the trees remains. We have taken the enchanted branches and fashioned our coracle, firmly fitting each breadth of wood against the next, and carved our oars with magical skill.

HP: (Holds out wood slips face down. Turns them over and distributes them.)

From the twigs we have shaped the sacred names upon its prow. We feel the firm wood upon which we rest, and the life still flowing through the slender branches which form our weapons.

HPS: *Wise to the weathers of fortune, we test the wind with a finger* (lick and raise middle finger) *as it sweeps across the flooding depths. Its whisper is heard above the splash of our oars.*

ODIN! POSEIDON! MELIAI! WODEN!

HP: *We have no fear of a watery grave, for we know our vessel is at home with the power of the sea, and that we sail with full speed straight at the heart of our destiny.*

(Circle members do not link hands this time. Each concentrates during the following on personal matters.)

. . . and echo the cry of the wind on the deep waters:

CIRCLE: *Isis! Athena! Thetis! Norn!*

HPS: *To the Ash is given directness of aim, far-reaching stability, the power of the sea, written characters, weather wisdom, dispensing of judgment, and the waters of rebirth.*

(HPS touches tip of middle finger to the left palm of each participant, closing fingers over the palm when finished.)

> *To us is given the Ash. It is our knowledge and awareness that gives it form for the world to see.*

(HPS writes Ogham Nion in center of right palm, facing outward, leaving palm open when finished.)

HP: *We must take care that we do not take on its cruelty, that we do not try to strangle paths of living which are not our own, that we do not keep from growth that which is around us, nor take justice unfairly in our own hands.*

HPS: *Of our purpose and our lives we must be able to say, "I am a wind upon the waters." We must temper the watery storms of emotion with the calm winds of logic and reason.*

FEAST OF THE ELEMENTS:

AIR: *The wind upon deep waters speaks, and we hear its message.*

(Air symbol is shared around the circle.)

FIRE: *Our energies guide our journey and defend the enchantment given to us.*

(Fire symbol is shared around the circle.)

WATER: *We ride the floods, knowing that with them comes rebirth.*

(Water symbol is shared around the circle.)

EARTH: *We replant in our lives the magic of the Ash.*

(Earth symbol is shared around the circle.)

HPS: *Night still reigns and the waters rise and storm about us. But rebirth approaches, and the Sun grows stronger — above us and within us.*

WORKING:
DISMISSAL OF THE SPIRITS:
THANKS TO THE DEITIES:
CIRCLE IS ENDED:

Fourth Moon: Alder

Quadrant guards are lighted as circle begins. Altar candles are soft shades of red or blues-shading-into-reds. Prepare red egg shells with soil and seeds already planted. Ogham marking tool is in place.

This is a Fire Moon; thus, the quadrants can be symbolized in fire. For example, a candle in a butterfly shape could be used at Air, a candle in a shell at Water, etc. The atmosphere and decor should still be somewhat stark, with only a hint of the profusion of growth and life to come.

About one week to ten days before the rite, rinse the egg shells broken for breakfast or baking, and save them. Dye them with red food coloring and a slight amount of water. Turn them upside down on a paper towel and let them dry.

Soak Moonflower or other seeds in warm (but not hot) water overnight, and nestle them into the shells which have been partially filled with potting soil. Cover with added soil, water well, and keep in a warm place until time for the ritual. The top of the water–heater is nicely warm and dark. Be sure that you check them daily and keep them moist (but not wet). The seeds will be ready to sprout during the week or so following the ritual and can be transplanted outdoors when they are a few inches tall; but they will not sprout before the rite.

If Moonflower seeds are not available, use green beans. These seeds sprout quickly, often within a week. Begin these seed cups only a few days before the ritual as you do not want them sprouted at the time of the rite. You may wish to prepare a few extra egg cups, as some seeds will invariably choose to sprout early.

The refrigerated Danish or orange rolls make quick and easy "Hot Cross Buns" which represent the breasts of the Earth Mother. Bake as

directed, but place the icing only in an "X" across the top rather than spreading it over the entire upper surface.

This is a perfect Moon during which to use Cointreau or a similar liqueur in the chalice, as the spicy, heated drink adds a touch of fire to the "wine." This blends with the inner flavor of this lunation.

If you or members of your group are recovering alcoholics or are abstaining for other reasons, the same effect can be obtained alcohol-free by mulling any appropriate fruit juice with cinnamon and cloves. Either form of "liquid fire" can be lightly heated just before the ritual to intensify the effect.

Alder
Moon of Utility

TEMPLE IS PREPARED:

WORKING IS PLANNED: This Moon is consistently a Fire moon. Work should be done related to energies and movements.

CAULDRON: hops, pennyroyal, sandalwood

CIRCLE IS CAST: Invitation/Invocation Casting

DEDICATION: Select Fire or solar deities for this Moon, such as Grainne, Oma-terasu, Bran, or Apollo

From the union of the Great Earth Mother and the Sun comes the birth of the universe and ourselves, their children. The Great Wheel turns once again to the season of Fire and rebirth. Thus we, as babies washed ashore from the womb of the Earth Mother, catch our breath as the swirling emotions which flooded our birth begin to lessen with the fire of the season. We begin to see beyond the tides which overwhelmed us, recognize the ebb and flow, and separate the waves which wash against the newness of our spirits.

HP: *Yet our emotions are just now settling into patterns which we can control. The Great Mother, knowing that Her Children are sometimes afraid of the dark, set a part of Herself in the skies to reflect the light of the Sun to the darkness, to reassure us. We see the Moonrise just beyond the now gentling waves. In that light, reflected within us as well as softly bathing our faces, we examine ourselves.*

HPS: *We examine our toes and the steps they take, our fingers and the things they do. We look within and find a struggling, pulsing part of ourselves responding to Her light and to our scrutiny, attempting to grow and burst from the restrictions we have established for ourselves within. The seed of our spirit shatters its encasement, putting out small feelers of ourselves, searching for nourishment. Here: in our thoughts; there: in our souls. Again, in our newly crystallizing emotions, and also in the reflexes of our bodies. We put out roots into the soil of Her Spirit.*

HP: *We look within, identifying the heritage we carry, determining what we would grow as an acorn knows itself and becomes an oak, as a seed kernel searches within to know that it is wheat, or corn, even as one plant knows to cling and climb, another to grow straight and sturdy.*

122

HPS: *It is not yet full Spring. At this time we are small sprigs and tiny shoots still examining and reaching to grow but not yet breaking through the surface to turn our faces to the light.*

HP: (Hands out egg cups with hidden seed in red shells.) *And thus the Wheel moves. Examine . . . Know. . . . Grow . . . and Become.*

(Circle joins, each holding their egg "cup" and charging the seeds within it. The chant is "Horus, Bast, Maat, Ra")

HPS: *I, the Great Mother, cherish the tendrils of spirit you send forth: reaching, touching, pressuring against my breast, my Horus-Children of the Earth.*

I understand your searching and give you my light by which to see and understand yourself.

I know your fears and hold you close and safe.

I know your needs and provide the grains for the strength of your bodies, rains for your thirst, and the source of my Spirit for your soul.

Know that in your struggles to grow, I am here, nourishing and nurturing, making room within my Spirit for the roots of all you are to be.

From the breasts of my Earth and the light of my love, grow strong in the strength of my Spirit.

(Cakes and Wine are shared)

To the Alder, a shining teardrop of the Sun, I give clarity, resurrection, and fire. To you, my children, I give the Alder (touches tip of ring finger to left palm of each participant, then draws the Fearn glyph or character in the right palm). *Your knowledge of yourself and the Alder within gives it form and expression in your life.*

HP: *Remember that you are the Earth Mother of your actions. You have planted your seeds of the season. Take care to nurture them with your efforts, your thoughts, and your love so that they, too, may grow strong, the fruitfulness of Her Spirit manifest in your harvest-to-be.*

WORKING: (Chant: "Evoe Bran, Ecco Argeia")
DISMISSAL OF SPIRITS:
THANKS TO THE DEITIES:
CIRCLE IS ENDED:

Fifth Moon: Willow

At the time of this Moon, the Willows may have not yet begun to leaf out and their branches become pliable. You may not be able to obtain adequate willow withes (branches). While Willow is specifically needed for making Willow wands, it is certainly easy enough and acceptable to utilize raffia or wicker weaving materials for circlets. Those craft-type materials are available at most comprehensive arts-and-crafts stores or centers.

Ribbon, or florist's tape, which can be purchased from a flower shop or a wholesale store, are quite handy to use for wrapping or tying the wreaths or circlets. These will hold them in the position or size you desire.

While many florists may not wish to sell tape, they frequently have remnants of a roll left, and they may give it to you or charge only a minimal amount. Using green or a natural color will depend on whether you plan to make your circlets from a natural or a peeled branch. If you prefer the peeled form, you may wish to ask for the neutral- or natural-colored tape.

CIRCLETS: Begin with the widest end of the Willow branch, curving it into a circle. Weave the more flexible, narrowing portion in and out around the main branch to provide more stability of shape and reinforcement of the circlet. After the first few "wraparounds," hold the position between the forefinger and thumb to adjust to your head size. When you have it properly sized, you may wish to fasten it at that point with a small amount of florist's tape or ribbon. If you'd rather not have other materials in your circlet, use the ribbon temporarily to hold the size while you continue working. Continue weaving the remainder of the willow withe around the main stem until the end of the branch is reached. Carefully slip the end of the willow stem between previous windings to fasten it securely into place, add tape or ribbon if you wish, and wear it for the remainder of the ritual.

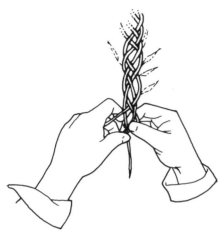

Braid just as with three strands, but use four (leaves left out of drawing for clairty).

Weave the ends back into the wreath. Flowers etc. may also be woven in.

Keep the Willow circlet as part of your magical equipment or accessories. For later uses, silk flowers can be fastened into place if desired, or fresh flowers may be woven into the basic circlet spacings.

WILLOW WANDS: Select the branch or withe desired (usually between one and two feet in length), and remember to ask the tree for its permission to take the branch.

You will need paring knives, your boline, or other scraping object. Begin peeling or scraping the outer bark of the withe to reveal the moist, pale inner wood. When you have it peeled to your satisfaction, cut it to the exact length you want.

Symbols may be written or carved into the bare wood during this rite. Such carvings are easier to make while the wood is fresh and moist. However, it may be preferable to make and charge the basic wand in this ritual and leave any remaining work for a later time, when the work can be done while you are alone.

Stones or crystals may be fastened to the tip of the wand according to personal preference. It is suggested that natural materials, such as leather strips, cotton, silk or linen strips, or jewelry-quality silver wire, be used for this wrap fastening.

In personal work during the remainder of the lunation, thoroughly oil the wand to prevent its drying out or cracking. While any natural oil, such as cottonseed, linseed, or virgin olive oil, is suggested, a substitute such as baby oil, mineral oil, or an essential oil appropriate to the purpose of the wand can be used. Typical furniture oil or heavy, greasy oils should be avoided.

When the wand is complete to your satisfaction, consecrate it at an appropriate phase of the Moon and begin working with it in your personal practice. It is not a bad idea to have a segment of a natural-fiber cloth in which to roll and store the wand when not in use.

Willow
Moon of Enchantment

TEMPLE IS PREPARED:

WORKING IS PLANNED: (It is a good idea to use this Moon's working time to strengthen the inner magic, or magical Will, within each covener, as well as within the Coven itself, rather than working magic meant to aid others.)

CAULDRON: white willow bark, lavender, angelica

CIRCLE IS CAST:

DEDICATION: Select deities from Earth gods and goddesses, or from those noted for magical skills.

The Great Mother moved through the season of fire, watching Her children grow, children of the forests and fields, skies and seas — Children of Her Earth. The soul-searching had been done: the ivy spiraled in its growth, the oak reached directly to the Sun, and new growth covered the Earth.

We, too, have examined ourselves, set our patterns, and begun to grow. We have stirred from the rest of winter and reached to the Sun, breaking through the hard crust of our own inaction.

HP: *We begin now to throw away dead habits and establish those which speed us to our growth, as a mother bird sweeps her nest clear of last year's loose grasses and twigs, freshening it for nesting.*

HPS: *The Fire Moon dried up the winter floods and allowed us to reach to the Sun. Yet, the Goddess guards our tender growth lest the fire of the Moon and the fire of the season consume us in their flames. She banks our fires with Earth so that our life-flames are directed, not burning out of control.*

HP: *It is now fully Spring — evident in vistas of the greens of tender shoots, adding color to the new horizons of our lives. We now focus our energies and move to accomplish our goals, stripping away the unusable, the worn, the no longer effective — in our minds, our homes, and our souls — to make way for new growth.*

HPS: *I am the Queen of Spring, Mother of the Willow. From the primordial depths of my womb-sea the Willow draws its life.*

The Willow tree is mine: as Hecate, Circe, Hera, Persephone. For from the death of winter comes the life of spring. I gave birth to Zeus in a cave near a Willow. The Wry-neck, Crane, and Thrush nest in its branches.

To the Willow I have given Monday, the Moon, and the magic of enchantment.

To you I give the Willow.

(HPS gives the Willow fronds to each person. She touches the tip of the little finger on the left hand, and draws the Ogham "S" in the palm of the right hand of each participant.)

FEAST OF THE ELEMENTS:

Breathe deeply of the enchantment of the Willow.

(Air symbol is shared.)

Blend your energies with the magic of this Moon to set in motion that which you desire.

(Fire symbol is shared.)

It is your understanding and expression of the Willow's magic that gives it form which the world can see, and by which you are known.

(Water symbol is shared.)

Share with the Crane the cakes of my inspiration. Drink deeply of my magic and my love about which the Thrush sings.

(Earth symbol is shared.)

HP: *Draw your life-fires from the season. Take guidance from this Earthen Moon. Become the Willow, rooted deeply in the Earth, dancing with the wind, singing harmony with the music of life. Seek the depths of the waters of love and give shelter to the inspiration of the Goddess within.*

The Willow is yours. Become its Enchantment.

(With Willow fronds at hand, each participant may take theirs and prepare a wand or a circlet during the chant. Polarized or balanced forms of "Lady Weave Your Circle" or "Lady of the Silver Magics" is suggested.)

DISMISSAL OF SPIRITS:
THANKS TO THE DEITIES:
CIRCLE IS ENDED:

Sixth Moon: Hawthorn

Altar tapers in this rite should be in the colors of the Hawthorn — deep greens and soft pinks. Another alternative would be those colors which represent, to you, cleansing or rededication. Use cleaning tools and utensils for the decoration of the circle. Place a broom across the doorway into the circle so that it must be stepped on or across to enter. To intensify the image of cleansing, establish a literal circle of thirteen cleaning items: for example, a scrub brush, a dust pan, a whisk broom, a dust rag. You can even use a nail brush or old toothbrush which you use for cleaning.

If you have access to tapes of environmental sounds or a recording of the winds, play it at just above audible level while the Winds speak in this ritual. This adds immeasurably to its impact. If you cannot locate such tapes or would prefer to make your own, then gather your recorder and tapes and head for an isolated ravine on a windy day. From the rattle of branches and sound of the wind down the course of the ravine, you should be able to record a usable tape of wind sounds.

SILVER WHISTLES: While actual silver whistles would be nice, most of us cannot afford them for ourselves, much less for an entire group. However, there is an effective and inexpensive alternative. Most variety or children's stores have packages of brightly colored plastic whistles for children's birthday parties. It is a simple matter to brush or spray them with a silver-colored paint. Common aluminum spray paint works quite well.

Place the whistles in a row on newspaper or discardable grocery bags. Stir or shake the container of paint thoroughly and brush or spray the top side of the whistles evenly. Allow the whistles to dry thoroughly. Roll each whistle approximately one-third of a turn and repeat the painting and drying process. The final turn and painting process should result in whistles

that are thoroughly, evenly silver in appearance. The same process is used for the tiny wooden whistles that are sometimes found in Oriental stores. Care should be taken to avoid spraying paint within the whistling chamber because of potential toxins within the spray.

This Moon is the Earth aspect of Air. If you do not wish to use the silvery whistles as tokens for this rite, check the local hobby shop for tiny decorative brooms. Any small item used in cleaning is an ideal token for this rite. If you opt for these tokens rather than whistles, eliminate the group whistle near the end of the rite. Mark the Ogham in the receiving hand with the miniature cleaning tool, and place it in the expressive hand.

MEDITATION: This ritual can be adapted to provide a time for group meditation; or one can use only a worship-rite format. Meditation in this ritual may be performed before the Feast of the Elements or during the working segment of the rite.

It is a good idea to discuss the focus before the ritual begins. If inner awareness and individual contact is more important, then leave the meditation within the framework of the ritual itself. An ideal place for it is after the HP statement of "Whistle up the Wind; the Goddess speaks," which occurs just before the Feast of the Elements. The wind sounds can also be used effectively here.

Should the group, however, decide that it desires knowledge, input, or instruction from the Goddess for a particular group purpose, then select that focus (healing, group purpose, how to handle a particular situation, a method to obtain specific knowledge, etc.) and schedule the time for "meditation" following the Elemental Feast.

If this approach is taken, it is strongly suggested that time be allowed following the close of the circle for a thorough discussion of what all members of the group have received in this meditation. Someone should take notes for the group. The combined input will probably be used in a later working.

Hawthorn
Moon of Restraint

TEMPLE IS PREPARED:

WORKING IS PLANNED: This is a Moon to clear away both spiritual and physical deadwood and old habits, or to clarify your dedication and focus.

CAULDRON: hawthorn berries, valerian, chamomile

CIRCLE IS CAST:

DEDICATION: Select from wind and knowledge deities for this rite. While not Celtic, the Winged Isis and Thoth bring vibrations which are highly harmonious to the purpose.

HPS: *The Season of Fire nears its end. It has accomplished its purpose. The sacred Spirit Fires of the God and Goddess have refined our emotions and lighted our soul-searching. Now, as the season draws to a close, our inner flames, which were banked with the Earth Moon just past, spring to life again in this Air Moon.*

We turn our efforts from the mental and spiritual cleansing and instinctively begin to center on our homes: sweeping, scrubbing, clearing out the unused and unusable to leave our environment clean. We now put our energies into the spring cleaning of our homes as we have been cleaning our hearts and mind in past Moons.

This we have done year after year, life after life. At this Moon have we always cleaned the Temples, purifying the sacred places we have dedicated to the Goddess and the God. As sacred sparks of Her Spirit, we are now prepared to blaze into full growth with the inspiration of Her Hawthorn Moon.

HP: *Air becomes our thoughts. Think back, remember and see the Great She Bear and the Little She Bear dancing in the worshipful throng. Hear the cries: "ARTEMIS! ARTEMIS!"*

CIRCLE: *ARTEMIS! ARTEMIS! ARTEMIS!*

HP: *Relive the Festivals: "MAIA! MAIA!"*

CIRCLE: *MAIA! MAIA! MAIA!*

HP: *The She Bears turn Her Great Mill; cursed marriages of May are protected by Her Hawthorn. The Goddess is ever with us. Even though we may not see Her, we can hear Her voice if we but call to Her:*

CARDEA! CARDEA!

CIRCLE: *CARDEA! CARDEA! CARDEA!*

CARDEA: *I am Cardea. As mortal children, you are not always ready to hear my voice, perhaps fearful of what I would say. Thus, you have characters and symbols with which to write and communicate, to preserve your lore and learning. Thus, my words are always with you, even in the silence.*

You, my human children, can become fretful with the silence, even though you are not yet ready to listen to my Voice.

I whisper to your soul in the rustling of the leaves; I sing songs of my love for you in feathered flights across my sky. Still, you listen at times without hearing and hear without understanding. I speak as the Maiden (blows small silver whistle once), as the Mother (blows silver whistle once), and as the Crone (blows silver whistle once). I but whisper and the Winds carry my voice to the limitless reaches.

Harken, then, my sons and daughters, to the Winds, my messengers.

(HP blows silver whistle three times.)

CARDEA: *EURUS! Great Wind of the East and south of East! Speak to my children of Knowledge and Understanding.*

EURUS: *There shall ye assemble, who are feign to learn all sorceries, who have not yet won my deepest secrets. To these shall I teach that which is as yet unknown.*

Know that all thy seeking and yearning shall avail thee not unless thou knowest the mystery: that if that which thou seekest thou findest not within thyself, thou shalt never find it without thee.

(HP blows silver whistle three times.)

CARDEA: *NOTUS! Great Wind of the South! Speak to my children of the Soul.*

NOTUS: *I am the Beauty of the Green Earth, the White Moon amongst the stars, the mystery of the Waters and the desire of the hearts of men. I call unto my Soul to arise and come unto me, for I am the Soul of Nature.*

(HP blows silver whistle three times.)

CARDEA: *ZEPHYRUS! Great Wind of the West! Speak to my children of Love and of Death.*

ZEPHYRUS: *For my Law is Love — unto all beings. For mine is the Cup of the Wine of Life, the Cauldron of Cerridwen, which is the Holy Grail of Immortality. From me all things proceed, and unto Me all things must return. I give the knowledge of the Spirit Eternal.*

(HP blows silver whistle three times.)

CARDEA: *BOREAS! Great Wind of the North! Speak to my children of Earth and of Living.*

BOREAS: *Behold, I am the Mother of All Things, and my love is poured out upon the Earth. And ye shall be free from all slavery. Behold, all acts of love and pleasure are my rituals. Therefore, let there be beauty and strength, power and compassion, honor and humility, mirth and reverence within you.*

CARDEA: *When you have need of my words, call to me thrice. My winds will speak my thoughts.*

(Gives silver whistles to each participant in circle.)

HP: *From Time Beyond, we have seen and worshipped our Goddess as the sliver of silver in the stars, the full flowing orb which lights the heavens, and as the aging crescent fading from our sight. Even in the Dark of Moon, when we cannot see Her face — She is near. We have but to call Her: the Winds speak in Her voice if we will just take the time to listen and to hear.*

Whistle up the Wind! The Goddess speaks!

(Circle members take up whistles and blow them three times. A slight pause is effective — before the next words are spoken.)

HPS: *Know that I have given to the Hawthorn the knowledge of restraints, cleansing, and rededication. My winds in its branches speak to you of that which you need to curb or eliminate from your life. They speak of* *the need to cleanse the temples, both those in which you worship and the temple-body in which you live.*

(HPS marks the receiving Ogham "H" in the receiving hand of each participant, closing the fingers over the marking as she completes the rune.)

To you, I give the Hawthorn. It is your knowledge and understanding of the Hawthorn within that gives it form and expression for the world to see.

(HPS marks the expressive, visible Ogham "H" in the expressive palm of each participant, leaving the fingers open.)

(MEDITATION TIME IF REQUIRED)
FEAST OF THE ELEMENTS:
WORKING:
DISMISSAL OF SPIRITS:
THANKS TO THE DEITIES:
CIRCLE IS ENDED:

Seventh Moon: Oak

Rich greens, or perhaps a mixture of green, Sun-gold, and tan, the colors of summer, serve well as altar candles. Use oak leaves or small oak twigs and branches to bound the circle or decorate the altar.

FIRE SEASON CANDLE: I simply used an egg-shaped votive container. They are sometimes called egg-cups, and can occasionally be obtained at garage sales or purchased in specialty shops that feature or emphasize cooking and serving accessories.

SEASON OF WATER SYMBOL: Any bowl will serve for the symbol of the Season of Water. I use a small silver serving bowl that had been a family heirloom. You need not use silver; in fact, a gold-colored or bronze one might be much more appropriate to the solar symbolism.

FUNERAL MASKS: Any set of masks will serve. If you just happen to have an exquisite pair that you or a family member selected on a world tour, that is wonderful. However, the masks can be handmade of painted cardboard or shield-shaped wood. They can also be purchased inexpensively in almost any costume or stage magic shop. Simply select one in black and the other in gold or white. They can be plain like the "bandit"; raccoon style; or as ornate as you, your imagination, and your pocketbook wish.

Garage sales sometimes have a mask or two, especially if the family having the sale is a military or teaching family. Many ceramic shops offer faces of various cultures available in both finished or unfinished pieces.

The bright mask can be placed prominently on the altar or to the south. The mask for the dark Sun has a symbolic strength when placed to the north and then moved to the altar.

137

HINGES: Most hardware or variety stores will offer packets which contain several small hinge sets in a bronze finish. Put the small nails or screws in a sandwich baggie (to prevent losing them), and spray or brush the hinges with silver paint.

There are usually four nails or screws per hinge set, which gently reinforces (without saying anything) the concept of the four solar passage points of the year, the equinoxes and solstices. You may wish to paint them with elemental colors.

I have found it practical to tear a small segment of masking tape for each participant and stick the tape pieces to something unobtrusive in the circle. After the nails have been given, and a moment allowed for considering all that they mean, I hand out the tape bits and proceed to secure my four nails to the piece I have. The circle usually follows my example, which prevents someone losing part of their set or stubbing a toe on tiny nails in the carpet. Another solution for this potential problem is to have small, zip-type plastic bags available and hand them out at this point. Each set of symbols can then be slipped inside one and be sealed shut. These are easily found following the ritual. Sometimes, I even use the small self-adhesive labels to identify each participant's bag. That way, everyone can easily find his or her own as they prepare to leave.

Oak
Moon of Strength

TEMPLE IS PREPARED:

WORKING: Since this is often considered to be a sacrificial Moon, many do
no working on this Moon.

CAULDRON: oak leaves, Irish oak moss, sage leaves

CIRCLE IS CAST:

DEDICATION: Janus, the two-faced god, and Cardea, who resides at the
hinge of the world, are ideal choices this Moon.

HPS: Solar Invocation
  (See example in Invocation Appendix)

HP: (Responds by lighting God Candle on Altar.)
  Lunar invocation
  (See example in Invocation Appendix.)

HPS: (Responds by lighting Goddess candle.)

DRAWING DOWN THE LUMINARIES:

HP: *The Season of Fire is ended.* (Snuffs egg candle of Fire season.)

HPS: *The mood and movement of fiery beginnings becomes the flow of deep
currents in the Season of Water* (pours water into bowl of the season).

*Our temples are cleaned, our homes are scrubbed, and growth continues
toward harvest in the strength of the Sun.*

(HPS holds gold mask lovingly for all to see, relinquishing it to the Maiden as
the HP turns to present the darker mask. The Maiden then places the gold
mask to the south.)

HP: *Tonight we celebrate a sacred union of the Goddess's Water Moon and the
Zenith of the Sun, as the Bright and Shining Lord turns in Her embrace to
show His darker face.*

(Picks up dark funeral mask and presents it to the HPS. She holds it a moment, as if gazing into the face of a new lover, then places it prominently on
the altar.)

*We sometimes forget that our Lord of Light (*Moves golden mask to the altar) *is also the Lord of Darkness. He is at once Himself and His darker twin. At this, His brightest moment, He is both the Bright and Shining and the Darkening Sun.*

HPS: *This sacred union we celebrate tonight is the eternal reminder of the duality within our spiritual natures. We are children of both the Moon and the Sun. We draw our strength and our life from both.*

Within the Oaken moon is the source of the Oak Kings legends. The oak is a symbol for strength. Its ancient names carry the meaning of the stout, secure door in languages throughout our world.

Thus the Oak King is the Door which looks in both directions of the year at once as does the Sun.

HP: *Yet, the Oak King does not move with the year on His own. The Goddess is the Hinge upon which the Door of the Year has the freedom to move. Without that union with Her, His strength is merely a solid wall, unmovable by the turning Wheel of the Year and the motion of the seasons.*

(HPS gives silver hinges to each celebrant, marking the receiving Ogham D in the receiving palm with the hinge before placing it in the hand.)

The Goddess is the beginning, the Creatrix of all that is, shaping the strength of the Bright and Shining Sun, Her child, to his maturity so that He is prepared to be Guardian of the World of Darkness.

All things are of Her, from Her, and return to Her. Thus . . .

HP: *The Oaken Moon*

HPS: *And the Heather Sun mark the movement of the year.*

HP: *I, as my Darker Brother, bound myself in the Heather wood. Yet, My Lady Goddess, who holds the keys to all things, freed me to live again.*

These golden nails represent that which imprisoned me, but which could not hold me against Her will.

(Gives brass nails for hinges, marking the expressive Ogham D in the transmitting palm before placing the nails in participants' hands.)

HPS: *Because the elements obey me, they fasten the Oaken Door to the Hinge of the Year. So in your hands are Air, Fire, Water, and Earth.*

The Sun moves slowly and passes through the Seasons. So also do these elements represent the Seasons of the Year.

With these, you close the distances between yourself and myself as the Celestial Hinge. Yet, I open that which is closed, as I removed the fastenings which bound my Lord into his Heather coffin.

HP: *Remember that We are in All things, and as Our Children, you have within you all that We are. Use it wisely, knowing that as We both are Bright and Shining as well as Darkening, so also do you reflect All that is, or was, or can be from that which is within you.*

HPS: *Celebrate with us, our union, and that which exists within us All.*

FEAST OF THE ELEMENTS:
DISMISSAL OF SPIRITS:
THANKS TO THE DEITIES:
CIRCLE IS ENDED:

Eighth Moon: Holly

DECORATING THE CIRCLE: Altar candles are grey and deep red. A green-grey altar cover is also appropriate. Any of the iron colors are most appropriate to the decor or accents for this Moon. You might also wish to drape the Goddess statue or the base of the Goddess candle with a brief length of brilliant scarlet red. Angular patterns and elongated darker accents also carry the mood of the Moon.

If you have access to branches of scarlet oak, they, too, can be most effective in adding to the atmosphere of the ritual. Place them in the center of the circle, at a slight distance from the cauldron (if used), or upon the altar. You may use the traditional American Holly, if you wish, but be aware that it is the Holly Oak which is the symbolic tree.

This is a warrior Moon. The presence of a sword, spear, or other "soldierly implements" would support the atmosphere of this lunation well, regardless of whether they are used in the rite.

IMPACT AND STAGE DRESSING: If there are men in the group, have them read the "I . . . " statements following the first comments of the High Priest. They are noted in the ritual as being spoken by the elements. You might write those statements on small slips of paper and give them to the men to read from at the proper time. If there are not enough male voices, don't despair; remember that Athena, Minerva, and Freya are love-and-battle Goddesses and are fully as fierce as any of the battle-gods!

SPEARS: When I first wrote this ritual, I had no idea what would be used for the "spears" that are given to Circle members. However, I found that the Chinese food stores usually have inexpensive packages of shish-ka-bob skewers made of wood, blunt on one end and pointed on the other. These not

143

only worked quite well in Circle, but the unused ones also came in handy later in the kitchen.

If the skewers are unavailable, check out your local garden supply store. They will often have slender, pointed "stakes" for propping or supporting small plants or house plants. The only real difference is that the skewers are smaller, less expensive, and more versatile. They are also more easily held in the hand during meditation than are the prop-stakes.

Holly
Moon of Unity and Protection

TEMPLE IS PREPARED:

WORKING: (This is a Moon for unified working against that which impedes or prevents unity of Spirit, inner strength, or higher love.)

CAULDRON: holly leaves, witch hazel, goldenseal

CIRCLE IS CAST:

DEDICATION: Select from the Dark-Twin gods and the Love-and-Battle goddesses such as Minerva, Freya, Morrigan, or Athena.

This is a time when the sharpened shadows, which have gathered close in the strength of the Sun, begin to lengthen once more. The deep green of Summer is touched by the iron-gray of battle as the darker twin of the growing Sun strengthens his supremacy. The starlings wheel in precision flights; the wild ass brays his triumph and rides the battlefield.

The scarlet terebinth guides the chariots through the opening flowers and the ripened barley. The scream of the Valkyries rises above the never-ending battle.

HP: *Look beyond the fray. See the Goddess, clad in Royal Scarlet between the warring suns, embrace them both. Her Child, grown to Lover, and the Tanist, Executioner of Her Love.*

This is the warrior Moon. The voices of Tannus, Jove, Thor, Jehovah, and Marduk roll and crash in the darkening sky.

I am a battle-raging spear.

AIR: *I am a spear that roars for blood.*

FIRE: *I embolden the spearmen.*

WATER: *I fly as a spearhead of woe to those who wish for woe.*

EARTH: *I am a giant, hewing down an army — taking vengeance.*

HPS: *In the thunder of the battle, I remain serene. In me is the knowledge that I do not choose. My two loves are one, as I am with them. United, they are a Knight of green armed with spears of Holly.*

145

I am, at once, that upon which one moves, and that for which the other slays. I remain responsive to the sensuous embrace of each as it is His time.

I birthed the sacred oak and loved Him to His prime. Now is the season of His darker twin. My love must be destroyed before I can once more give him birth and move again to His embrace.

To the Bloody Holly Oak I give vengeance and the swift flight of the battle-driven chariot. Within its life-force I place the unerring thrust of a barbed spear and the strength of unity in purpose. To it I also give the strength of sensuous desire.

To you, My Children, I give the Holly Oak.

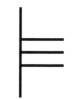

(HPS touches first digit of her middle finger to the palm of each participant's left hand. She draws the glyph of Tinne, the Ogham T, in that palm and closes the fingertips of that hand over the invisible rune.)

It is your knowledge and understanding of the Bloody Oak within that gives it form and expression which the world can see.

(Draws a visible Ogham Tinne in the open palm of the right hand of each member of the Circle, leaving the palm open when finished.)

HP: *Know the Bloody Holly Oak within you. Draw upon its strength and unity of purpose. Fear not to take aim when needful. Hurl the target-seeking spear against that which serves the darkness.*

Yet, be ye ever mindful! When the craze of battle lust is upon you and the sight of the target dims in the lessening light, Vengeance can be a dark ass that can be ridden to the death.

(As he speaks above, the HP gives each participant a "spear.")

(HPS begins chant: "Cerridwen, Athena, Freya" or "Janus, Cerridwen, Thor." Each participant concentrates on that within him- or herself which needs to be overcome.)

HPS: *Share with me the Feast of the Elements at this Holly Moon.*

Share with me the fragrance of the blossoms opening within us even in the midst of battle.

(Air symbol is shared around the circle.)

Share with me the blazing courage of the spearman standing fast in the heat of battle.

(Fire symbol is shared around the circle.)

> *Share with me the Love which transcends Time and Vengeance and the Unity which expresses it even as the battles rage.*

(Water symbol is shared around the circle.)

> *Share with me the strength of the spear-arm as the call to battle comes.*

(Earth symbol is shared around the circle.)

DISMISSAL OF THE SPIRITS:
THANKS TO THE DEITIES:
CIRCLE IS ENDED:

Ninth Moon: Hazel

CIRCLE DECOR: Altar candles are brown and bright orange, or red and silver. The altar cloth or cover, if one is used, should be brown. Place a flat, circular mirror (several inches in diameter) in the center of the circle. Surround the edges with small plants or greenery. Small statues of the Pegasus or Unicorn are ideal within the greenery. If you have and use both, place the Pegasus somewhat in the open and partially conceal the Unicorn with a branch or trailing portion of some of the plants. An apple should be nestled in the edge of the plant nearest the unicorn. A bowl with a silvery inner finish will also serve well to present the image of a secret or hidden pool.

If possible, place a single potted house plant with somewhat taller stem or trunk near one edge of the greenery-surrounded mirror or bowl. It is especially appropriate if you can turn the plant so that one branch sticks out over the bowl.

HAZEL NUTS: These are another item which can be purchased during the holiday season at the end of the year and frozen to be used at Hazel Moon. Any nuts still in their shells would serve, but the freezer makes using real hazel nuts easy.

I usually conceal the collection of hazel nuts (nine for each participant, including myself) under the edge of the cloth at the altar, or under the greenery near where I will be sitting (normally at the East facing West or in the South facing North). Nine hazel nuts can be unobtrusively gathered up as the Muse is being called. At the point in the ritual where the Muse speaks of the kernels falling into the Hippocrene Spring, they can be "dropped" into the "pool" if you have used a bowl of water as the pool. Otherwise, quietly place them on the surface if the mirror is the apparent "spring." They can be dropped here, as well, but the hard sound of the impact on the mirror is distracting and discordant, while the soft splash is harmonious to the tone of the Moon.

THE APPLE: Have an apple for each person who will be in the circle. If you prefer each participant to experience the concept thoroughly, place an added knife in the circle, cut your apple, and then pass the knife around so that each person halves his or her own apple at that point in the ritual.

As an alternative, before the ritual you may wish to cut each apple carefully in half. Make the cut horizontal (around the circumference of the fruit, not stem to base) in order to show the star formed by the seed placements. Dip the cut surfaces in lemon juice. This will reduce the tendency of most fresh fruits to quickly turn a darker color and present an unappetizing appearance. Then, replace the halves snugly together. Position the apples around the altar at the approximate locations where members will be sitting. They should be cut only moments before the ritual begins.

Cut the apple as directed, showing the star centers to circle members. Identify the two halves as the two stars visible from the Earth, as indicated in the ritual. Take time to glance at the apple halves before you show them, so that the the seed stars are properly positioned to point upward.

As a fresh apple is somewhat juicy, it might be a good idea to have a damp rag or paper towel within reach. A well-dampened wash rag can be placed on a square of waxed paper near the altar or hidden just beneath the altar cloth if one is used. My personal feeling is that the actual cutting of the apple is most important. Unfortunately, the lingering stickiness which results could detract from later parts of the ritual.

THE OGHAM MARKINGS: Because of the longer-than-usual statement about the tree, and the use of two trees, it may be better to complete the statements about the gift of the trees and then move to mark both trees in the receptive hands of the participants. Pausing briefly between the hazel and the apple glyphs is a good idea. In that pause, establish a moment of eye contact with the circle member before placing the other rune in the hand.

By presenting the inner gift of the runes in this manner, you do not have to repeat the meaning, and you make each gift very personal and intense for each member of the circle. This also allows a brief time of silence in which the participants can consider and absorb the gift while you complete the circle.

APPLE SEEDS: As Q're speaks of sharing the wisdom and considering the kernels of truth, the HPS or Maiden should obviously begin removing the apple seeds from her halves of fruit. A simple motion to follow that example is usually adequate to have the circle members remove their seeds as well. Hold the seeds for charging in the chant which follows. Some participants may simply eat all of their apple, including the seeds!

FEAST OF THE ELEMENTS: The apple half can be used for Air, as the fragrance should still be quite evident. Frequently, a candle store will have fairly small and inexpensive apple-shaped candles available. These would be excellent for the Fire symbol. For this Moon, I usually have two chalices and pass them both. One contains apple juice, the other Frangelico (or another hazel-nut liqueur). Small salmon-balls are my choice for Earth in this ritual because of their symbolism, and because the silent impact of eating the salmon, and eating of the knowledge, will remain with each participant. If you are not accustomed to making the salmon balls or croquettes, an easy method can be found in the "Recipes" in Appendix D.

Hazel
Moon of Wisdom

TEMPLE IS PREPARED:
WORKING IS PLANNED: This is a Moon best spent with adequate time
  for personal meditation on inner wisdom rather than active
  working on externals.
CAULDRON: star anise, catnip, ivy leaves
CIRCLE IS CAST:
DEDICATION: Q're and Artemis Caryatis are suggested, but any of the
  wisdom and inspiration deities will do.

As the ninth Moon emerges from the Dark Womb of the skies, its beginning
light reveals a Sacred Grove.

We see the shimmering white of a great steed and bright sparks from
silvered hooves dancing upon the mountain. Music echoes in our minds with
the beat of the giant wings. With one last flashing stamp of its hoof, the
winged horse rises into the air with another fragment of poetry, conveying it
to the starry heavens.

That last silvered stamp of a singing hoof creates a sacred spring which fills
the hollow made by its force. Perhaps . . . could it be . . . that we stand upon
Mt. Helicon? Could that truly have been the Pegasus we saw take flight?

HP: *Let us call to the Muses and let their inspiration clear our vision so that
we may clearly see where we are:*

  CALLIOPE! (kuh LIE uh pea)

(Circle echoes each Muse name three times.)

  CLIO! (KLEE oh)

(Circle echoes the name.)

  ERATO! (eh RAH toe)

(Circle echoes the name.)

  EUTERPE! (you TER pea)

(Circle echoes the chant.)

>*MELPOMENE! (mel po MEAN ee)*

(Circle echoes the name.)

>*POLYHYMNIA! (pahl ih HIM nnee uh)*

(Circle echoes the name.)

>*TERPSICHORE! (terp sih CORE a)*

(Circle echoes the name.)

>*THALIA! (THAY lee uh)*

(Circle echoes the name.)

>*URANIA! (you RAHN ee uh)*

(Circle echoes the name.)

MUSE: *Look before you, Mortals, and behold the first upthrust sprig of the Hazel tree. Into its heart, my sisters and I pour all knowledge of the arts and sciences, eloquence and beauty. Days and moons pass. The Hazel Moon comes again and then a third time, then thrice and thrice again.*

Now its branches reach high into the air and arch gracefully over the welling spring below. Among the whispering leaves are the swelling buds of its first year of fruit. The heavy-laden branches loosen their harvest, and the kernels fall, each filled with all knowledge and eloquence, into the crystal clarity of the Hippocrene Spring.

Ah! Your mortal mind thinks them wasted, but look you once more upon the spring. The sacred salmon gather the nuts which have fallen into their domain and eat of all Wisdom, and all Beauty.

Hearken, Mortal — The Salmon speaks with the voice of Q're.

Q'RE: *When the Pegasus is in flight and wings beyond our vision, and the salmon hide the fruit of the Hazel, I give you the Wild Apple beneath which the companion of the Pegasus takes shelter. Look closely now and see that shimmering presence beneath the laden branches. As it rests, its golden horn dislodges the ripened fruit. Hold the harvest of the Tree of Immortality through Wisdom, the Poet's salvation, and discern my Mother's presence.*

(Chant is Venus, Olwen, Eve.)

(HPS holds up an apple and cuts it in half horizontally. She holds both halves up with the seed center facing the members of the circle.)

HPS: *I am Artemis Caryatis, Moon Mother of the Nut tree. Part this companion fruit as the Sun parts the skies in its journey and find my presence at Birth, as Maiden, Mother, Crone, and Guardian of the Grave from which you are reborn.*

(In front of each member of circle should be an apple [see the preparation information on choice of when to cut them]. The HPS indicates these apples and has each member of the circle pick theirs up. She separates hers and holds the cut face toward the participants so that the stars formed by the seeds or seed pockets are visible.)

> *In your left hand is my starry symbol from the Earth, Hesper, the evening star which lights the darkness. In your right is Lucifer, Son of Morning, promise of the day to come.*

> *To the Hazel, Tree of Wisdom and Inspiration, the Poet's tree, I give Wednesday, the Nine Muses, the wings of Mercury and Pegasus for the poetry of words, movement, and song.*

> *I place the Hazel within you . . .*

(HPS touches the left palm of each member of the circle, marking a non-visible Ogham "C" in it with her finger before closing the participant's fingers over their palm.)

> *. . . that it may be shared.*

> *To the Apple, Tree of Immortality through Wisdom, I give the purity of the Unicorn, Friday, and Venus, that immortality is expressed in love and beauty as well as in wisdom. Within you I place the means of expressing the timelessness of that wisdom.*

(She touches left hand of each participant in the same manner as with the Hazel, but using the Ogham "Q", again closing their fingers over their palm.)

> *When you share and express these wisdoms, they become the hidden forms of what the world sees.*

(Marks the Coll and Quert letters visibly in the right palm, leaving the palm open when she completes both letters.)

Q'RE: *The seeds of Wisdom come in many forms. Some fall into the Hippocrene pool within our minds and are at once absorbed. Others fall upon the earthen ground of our conscious minds and seasons may pass before the birth of understanding. Wisdom hoarded selfishly produces* *bitter and poisonous fruit as the Dripping Hazel Tree deals death rather than wisdom at its inspiration.*

Thus I, Q're, charge you to share the wisdom you are given and to take the time to consider the kernels of Truth you receive. In this manner your wisdom grows with understanding. The loving gift of it becomes Immortal.

(Apple seeds are removed — Chant: "Evoe, Q're, Ecco Caryatis")

HPS: *Share with us the immortal thoughts of wisdom.*

(Air symbol is shared.)

Share with us the eternal illumination of wisdom.

(Fire symbol is shared.)

Share with us the ever-changing beauty of wisdom.

(Water symbol is shared)

Share with us the ever-present source of wisdom, Life itself.

(Earth symbol is shared)

HP: *When you search for the light of wisdom and find it not, remember that you ARE the Sacred Grove. Within you grows the Hazel and the Apple. Sheltered there within you are the spirit and expression of that Wisdom. Within you is the skill of sharing its Truth.*

When you ask, despairingly, "But where is wisdom . . . and where is understanding?", recall the gifts of the Goddess this night and know that Wisdom shall be found under the Apple Tree within you:

. . . found in the patterns of your mind, on a day you honor the goddess of love, and when the Moon shines full in the sky. . .

And the finder shall be the Winged Messenger within you.

DISMISSAL OF SPIRITS:
THANKS TO DEITIES:
CIRCLE IS ENDED:

Tenth Moon: Vine

Altar candles are the multi-colored candles that are designed to drip wax. Some are called "rainbow-dripping candles" and are used with wine bottles. Continue the variegated color scheme with the altar cover, if one is used.

TONE AND ATMOSPHERE: If you can utilize a tape recording of haunting, minor-mood flute music for the beginning of the ritual, and can leave it running at just-audible levels for the remainder of the rite, you will greatly enhance the feeling of this Moon.

DECOR: Ideally, the circle is formed or bounded with grapevines. However, if you have no access to the natural vines, you could utilize some of the excellent silk examples available at many variety stores, or trail twists of hemp or twine (offered at most hardware stores) to simulate the vines.

Small bunches of red and green grapes should be placed at the North of the circle (at Earth) and on the altar. Other symbols of the harvest season are appropriate. Colored gourds, brightly colored ears of corn, fruits, and vegetables (available at this time in most grocery stores) will heighten the mood of this Moon, and will add vibrancy to the visual images.

WINE CUPS: Although a single chalice can certainly be used, the impact of this Moon is most deeply felt when each member of the circle has his or her own "wine cup." This can easily be done by using the small, juice-size glasses or clear plastic throwaway cups (old-fashioned size). Many grocery stores and most liquor stores will carry the disposable wine glasses. These will serve beautifully for this Moon.

Pour a small amount of wine in each cup and proceed through the gifts of the wine to the senses. The musical sound of the wine cups meeting is more effective with the small "real" glasses than with the plastic cups.

For the portion of the ritual which works through the First to Third Grapes, pour only a sip into each cup, or just enough for one swallow. Then, with the offering of the "New Wine of the Season," pour a reasonable serving for each member. While the "new wine" is not usually drunk during the season it is made, it is toasted upon harvest and when it is released as a full wine. It is this toasting moment — the salute to the wine's potential — which is presented here.

CIRCLETS: These circlets of vine are made in the same manner as the Willow circlets. You will find instructions for making crowns or circlets in the section on the Willow Moon.

MARKING THE RUNES: Consider marking the runes in both hands with the tip of a finger moistened in the wine, rather than with an actual visible mark.

FEAST OF THE ELEMENTS: This is an easy Moon in which to use some form of wine at each quadrant. A small bowl of a very fragrant wine or liqueur (peach, perhaps) serves well at Air, especially if slightly heated to release a stronger fragrance. A very clear, golden wine or spicy liqueur represents Fire. A rosy- or blackberry-type wine in the Chalice works nicely, and of course, you already have the grapes at Earth.

Be as dramatic as you wish with this Moon; it can handle it. After all, Bacchus is the god of wine, and the Bacchanalia is still worth celebrating.

Vine
Moon of Exhilaration

TEMPLE IS PREPARED:

WORKING IS PLANNED: (An excellent Moon to work for the specific knowledge or inspiration needed for each individual, whether for a solution, a direction, a concept, or method.)

CAULDRON: uva ursi leaves, valerian, lemongrass

CIRCLE IS CAST:

DEDICATION: Dionysus or Bacchus, and Aridella.

The flame of the Sun is tempered by the turning of the wheel. Its fiery kiss ripens the fruits of the Earth. We see about us the abundance of harvest.

It is the vintage season. We have shared the fragrances of the vine in springtime, the heat of summer ladening its branches, and now prepare ourselves to receive the new wines of the autumn harvest.

(HPS turns on recorder with tape of soft flute music, subtly increasing volume as HP speaks.)

HP: *We wander through the vineyards, finding that our steps keep rhythm with the echoes of piping heard in the distance. That primal beat stirs our summer-lazy bodies and we dance upon the pathway attuned to the Dance of the Year and the Spin of our Destinies.*

(HPS or Maiden slowly increase the volume of the flute music as HP speaks.)

The piping grows louder as we follow it to its source and behold a Sacred Grove profuse with the vine and hidden by the bramble.

HPS: *We see Bacchus regally enthroned, Aridella by his side, Satyrs filling his wine cup, and nymphs moving with the sensuous piping.*

Let us join them and share in the joy of the first wine of the season.

(Gives each participant a wine cup as HP "uncasks" the "new" wine.)

HP: *The new wine flows smoothly mellow even before its proper season, and we understand why the vine is the tree of joy and exhilaration.*

HPS: *Behold the harvest of my springtime blossoms, the passion of His Summer Sun.*

159

(Holds wine cup to light.)

> *There is Beauty and Joy to see . . .*

(Smells the wine.)

> *. . . There is Pleasure and Delight in its fragrance . . .*

(Tastes the wine.)

> *. . . There is Exhilaration in its taste . . .*

(Touches her glass audibly to HP's glass.)

> *. . . And there is an echo of the pipes to awaken our memory.*

HP: *The bramble is a heady draft, and at times, the faerie spirit makes itself known through it.*

> *It can also form a crown of thorns through your actions and is difficult to wear. So drink with enjoyment, not excess.*

(Maiden pours a small sip into each wine cup.)

HPS: *My Children, Taste: Of the First Grape.*

> *Know that in it there is joy, pleasure, and delight for the senses and the Spirit.*

(Maiden pours a taste into each wine cup.)

HP: *Taste: Of the Second Grape.*

> *Know that in it there is the exhilaration of drunkenness, of feeling stronger, mightier than you truly are.*

(Maiden pours a taste into each wine cup.)

HPS: *Taste: Of the Third Grape.*

> *Know that in it are the dregs, the wrath of the Vine and the Bramble, and the pains of regrets.*

(HPS pours a generous measure into each wine cup.)

> *For you, My Children, I offer Wine of the Season. Drink deeply of the First Grape only.*

(HP and HPS salute each other, then touch glasses with each circle member, then sip the wine.)

HP: *The Vine grows anew each Spring and brings the Kiss of the Sun to the Vintage Season, eternally the same, ever anew.*

We were there when the Vines were planted.

CIRCLE: *Ho! Dionysus!*

HPS: *We have tended the Vineyard through Time.*

CIRCLE: *Hail! Osiris!*

HP: *We now share in the uncasking of the New Wine of the Season.*

CIRCLE: *Ho! Bacchus!*

HPS: *The Vine Moon is here once more.*

(Each person takes the grape vine nearest them and holds it. HP/HPS begin the chant.)

> *Blood of the Ancients Flows through my veins. The forms pass . . . But the Circle of Life remains!*

(Each member makes a circlet of the vine for him- or herself)

HP: *The Vine is, in its fruits*

HPS: *The Cup and the Flame . . .*

HP: *. . . The Breeze and the Earth.*

(HPS or Maiden mark the invisible Ogham Muin in the receiving hand of each partici-pant.)

HPS: *You, my Children, are my Wine of all Seasons. I charge you to give to your world, through your actions and your thought, the beauty, joy, ex-hilaration and music of the First Grape only.*

(Ogham Muin is marked in the transmitting palm.)

FEAST OF THE ELEMENTS: (Fragrant wine at Air; golden-white at Fire; Blackberry wine at Water; and grapes at Earth.)

DISMISSAL OF SPIRITS:
THANKS TO DEITIES:
CIRCLE IS ENDED:

Eleventh Moon: Ivy

DECOR AND MOOD: Altar candles are deep green. The altar cover is blue. Trails of ivy should encircle the altar arrangement. This, like the tenth Moon, is one in which the boundary of the circle can be easily marked by its symbol, the ivy. If you have potted plants which have even a couple of feet of tendrils or trailing branches, space them about the circle to create the effect of boundaries. Sometimes, a neighbor who has the Hedira Helix twining the trees and bordering the flower beds will be more than happy to offer you some of the profuse growth; it never hurts to ask. You could also begin in the spring, purchasing several Hydera Helix ivies from the local nursery and promoting their growth with extra energies, crystals in the pot, and ordinary fertilizer. You will have a built-in supply that beautifies your home in the interim.

Although it does require a bit of extra effort, artfully placing a container of dry ice in the area of the circle certainly aids in creating a hazy atmosphere appropriate to this Moon. Place deep-toned autumn leaves about the circle. Mushrooms should be placed on the altar and at Earth. Small pumpkins and similar items of late harvest are suitable decoration and enhancement of the mood of this Moon.

Playing a conch shell horn or a tape of a hunting horn just before the High Priest speaks for the first time heightens the impact of the ritual. If you can locate the white-leafed ivy, it should be placed on the altar in the center. Small evergreen branches (approximately the length of the hand) and strands of ivy should be gathered to the altar as well. There should be enough mini-branches and ivy strands to allow one to each participant.

Only two of the elements lend themselves to obvious symbols. If you can obtain a legal ivy ale or ivy wine, wonderful; if not, use one of the five-pointed herb leaves which are suitable for consumption and make a tea for the chalice. Large, ordinary mushrooms at Earth easily suggest the amanita and the bassarids. For Air and Fire, use your imagination and see what symbols you can devise that enhance the Feast of the Elements for you and your group.

A point to consider discussing (perhaps after the ritual when everyone can look at their palms) would be the fact that the Gort rune reads the same whether turned inward to the circle member or outward to the world. This is in harmony with the fact that joys and regrets can turn into each other so quickly, just as the enjoyment of the wine can so easily become over-indulgence that leads to regret. You might even ask that each Circle member examine his or her life between the time of the ritual and the next meeting to identify points of his or her life which are on that edge between joy and regret, and what action might be needed to avoid the regret.

Ivy
Moon of Exhilaration

TEMPLE IS PREPARED:

WORKING IS PLANNED: This is a time to find those areas and levels of fierceness within. They serve as a strength and a defense. Identify also those which could too easily go beyond defense and strength to render harm to yourself or others.

CAULDRON: ivy leaves, elder flowers, orange blossoms

CIRCLE IS CAST: Quadrant guards are unlighted.

DEDICATION: Artemis and Tammuz; or select from other goddess/boar-killed lover-deity pairs.

The November rains have not yet begun. The blue of the autumn skies reflects in the haze upon the hillsides and the smoke of autumn fires. The mute swan follows the whistling swan into the skies as the roebuck travels the forest. The wild boar is hunted through the glens, and a tardy gleaner reaps the Harvest Bride. It is the time of the Mysterion. Toward the polestar, the amanita flaunts its scarlet beneath the Birch and calls to the Bassarids.

HP: *The horns of the hunt and revelry are sounded. Bacchanalia begins and the quarry moves with the hunters.*

(HP moves around the circle in short steps, looking around and over his shoulder as a fugitive might, playing the part of the wild boar. As he pauses briefly at each quadrant, the person for that element speaks and lights the quadrant guard. As the element speaks, the "Boar" is startled and moves on. Each element should allow a moment to elapse between the previous one and the boar comment to come.)

AIR: *A bristly boar seen in a ravine.*

(Lights Air quadrant guard.)

FIRE: *A fierce boar.*

(Lights Fire quadrant guard.)

WATER: *A ruthless boar.*

(Lights Water quadrant guard.)

EARTH: *A ravening boar roving the hills.*

(Lights the Earth quadrant guard.)

(HP returns to the East and pauses there.)

HPS: *The beast of death has come full circle and now the hunter is the hunted. The boar is the Ivy. We seek its gaiety and rejoice, forgetting the Ivy's strength as the wine flows.*

HP: *However, there are those who remember the ravening beast waiting in its draft to take revenge:*

Artemis! Grainne! Aphrodite!

Her fury is unspoken, but the snow-tinted leaves of the ivy have hidden the sounds that she will not utter. From its ivied nest the gold-crest wren calls the names of those She loved.

Tammuz! Diarmuid! Ancaeus!

Her tears begin to flow and the rains begin.

HPS: *To the Ivy I give flowers when all around is dying. In its upward spiral is my promise of continuation and the choice to climb and spiral or to strangle other growth. To the Ivy I give the joys of intoxication and the regrets of ruthlessness.*

To you, My Children, I give the Ivy.

(Touches palm of left hand with the forefinger, marking an invisible Ogham "G" in the palm, and closes the fingers over it.)

It is your understanding and expression of the Ivy within you which gives it form the world can see.

(Marks a visual Gort in open palm of right hand.)

HP: *Do not forget the sorrow of the Goddess. Wreathe your ship of life with Her Ivy and stalk as a boar or a lion those who would steal away that which is your due.*

(HPS gives each member a small "fir" branch; HP gives tendrils of Ivy. The circle members then twine their "fir" branch with the Ivy.)

That which is unspoken is still remembered and is concealed in the strength of the Ivy's wine.

CHANT: *Evoe Artemis! Ecco Tammuz!*

HPS: *Share with me the Feast of the Elements in this Ivy Moon.*

*Share with me the intoxication of the Ivy and the Amanita, the silence of
the Goddess, and the cunning of the boar.*

(Air symbol is shared around the circle.)

*Share with me the fierceness of the Boar and the Bassarids, the fury of
the Goddess and the strength of Her love.*

(Fire symbol is shared around the circle.)

*Share with me the joys and sweet sorrow of loving and the regrets of ruth-
lessness and revenge, all bound within the Ivy.*

(Water symbol is shared around the circle.)

Share with me the power of the Ivy and strength of the Boar.

(Earth symbol is shared.)

WORKING:
THANKS TO THE DEITIES:
DISMISSAL OF THE SPIRITS:
CIRCLE IS ENDED:

Twelfth Moon: Reed

CIRCLE SETTING OR DECOR: This is a Moon of silence. Only the description of the season and the Moon is verbalized. All else is done in silence.

ALTAR: The low central altar should have four elemental altar tools: Incense, Sacred Flame, Chalice, and Cakes and Salt. If small owl magnets or other small, inexpensive owl motif items are available, they can be placed around the altar. The Altar candles are deep browns and the altar cover is green. The Circle is consecrated to Athena, Love-Battle-Wisdom Goddess of the Greco- Roman cultures, to whom the owl is sacred. Ideally, the candles are placed in owl candle-holders, but this is not a necessity.

This is an ideal Moon to utilize tall reeds to form a physi- cal circle boundary. If actual reeds are used, it is best to harvest them in July or August. Cut them and seal them by spraying with clear acrylic spray or heavy hair spray. This will prevent the scattering of the cattails as they ripen. These decorative reeds are also available at many florist shops or Oriental import stores. If that type of reed is not available, any of the same type of long leaves or plumes of Pampas grass may be used.

LIGHTING: The only light in Circle as participants enter should be the four quadrant guards and the Sacred Flame in the center of the Circle. The Circle is cast in complete silence. Invocations are also done silently. Only the description of the season and Moon (before the meditation time) is spoken aloud. The Feast of the Elements and Closing are performed in silence.

Reed
Moon of Security

TEMPLE IS PREPARED:
WORKING IS PLANNED: This ritual is in itself an inner working. Adding physical-plane work may negate or interfere with the internalization of the silence.
CAULDRON: seaweed kelp, hyssop, coriander
CIRCLE IS CAST:
DEDICATION: Athena, Serket or Hecate, and Pan.

The Season of Death grows more evident. The wind rises and keens a dirge for a dying world. The days are shorter; the light of the Sun grows weaker. Its warmth is vanishing, and its rays are edged with cold.

Instead of the sparkle of dew, our eyes meet the harsh glare of frost when we arise. The colors of Life have faded, and our Earth is drab and sere. The darkening year affects our spirits, and we fear the coming dark.

HP: *Sources of food are no longer evident in the fields. Animals scurry away from the encroaching cold to the warmth of their nests and dens.*

In earlier times we gathered reeds and re-thatched our homes to insure ourselves of snug warmth in the Deep of Winter.

We no longer thatch the roofs of our houses, but we strengthen our spiritual homes to preserve the light and warmth of our Inner Souls through the Season of Cold. Thus, we shall greet the return of Life from our spirit's shelter beneath the royal scepter of the Reed.

HPS: *It is the Season of Death. Listen to the silence of the Season, and you may hear the owl cry your name.*

It is the Dark of Sun—and a Moon of Silence.

Listen to the silence of this Moon.

Listen to the silence.

Listen . . .

MEDITATIVE TIME: (Allow appropriate time (*x* number of heartbeats, for example), or set a number of minutes, then silently call members back to active participation. This can easily be done by simply touching the person nearest, greeting them with a smile, and nodding toward the next participant. Thus, each person in circle gently touches and silently calls the next member back to physical consciousness and participation.)

PLACEMENT OF THE OGHAM: (Another approach to end the meditation time would be to silently take the receptive hand of the nearest participant and place the Ogham NG in the hand. Mark the out-going Ng in the other palm. When all in Circle have their silent letter, then begin the Feast of the Elements.)

SILENT FEAST OF THE ELEMENTS: (Allow a bit more time for this segment than you might use normally. Without the spoken preface to each element, some people will need added time to "tune in" to each of the symbols and truly share them.)

SILENT DISMISSAL OF SPIRITS:
SILENT THANKS TO DEITIES:
CIRCLE IS ENDED:

Thirteenth Moon: Elder

SETTING: Because it is a death Moon, or sacrifice Moon, the predominant color is black, both for altar candles and altar cloth. In the beginning, the temple is lit only by the light from outside the doorway. The quadrant guards are unlighted. In the center of the circle is a small skeletal figure (the paper cut-out with brads from Halloween is just right), shrouded by a square of black cloth. Before it is a small, unlit votive candle.

Glue the Halloween decoration on stiff poster board and cut it out. It will then stand on its own when wedged into a support base of Play-Doh or other clay. A scrap of filmy black fabric attached at the crown of the "head" allows it to be completely covered until the moment when it is revealed. Place the figure and votive cup on a lazy-susan turntable from the kitchen spice shelf. The rotating base makes it possible to slowly turn the figure to face each person in the circle while they hear the words about facing death.

Decorations around the circle should be somber and stark. Pomegranates, dried leaves, bare branches, and other "dead and wintry" items will work well. If the element symbols can be those which illustrate the Life-in-Death principle, so much the better. For example, Air could be a feathery airborne seed pod; Earth, an open pomegranate showing its seeds; Fire might be embers surrounded by or in a bed of ash. For Water, a simple bowl full of water with a dried leaf floating in it would be an example of this Moon.

TOOLS: You will need the marker for inscribing the Ogham rune, and small white feathers. A tape of wind sounds can be very effective here, as it was in the sixth Moon ritual. Having it play quietly, as the circle is cast helps to create the desired atmosphere. If the volume is gradually increased just before the first words are spoken, the reference to howling winds will be

173

enhanced. Maintain the volume for a moment, then slowly decrease it as the temple door closes and other thoughts are shared by the High Priestess or Maiden.

WORKING: Traditionally, no working is done on this Moon, which is considered a sacrifice Moon.

Elder
Moon of Completion

TEMPLE IS PREPARED:
WORKING: Traditionally, no working is done on this Moon, which is considered a sacrifice or death Moon.
CAULDRON: elder flowers, wild cherry bark, eucalyptus
CIRCLE IS CAST:
DEDICATION: Select from the Death or Guardian deities.

The wind howls in terror and slashes with icy sharpness.

(Temple door is slowly closed while the following is spoken.)

The Sun darkens, increasing our fears.

Violent emotions crash against our spirits. Depression attacks with a vengeance.

In a dark night of the soul which drags on, sometimes filled with despair, we stand face to face . . .

   . . . with Death.

(Maiden counts to thirteen silently, then lights the small votive candle. Removing the shroud over the figure, she slowly turns the figure to face each participant.)

HP: *We look into the eyes emptied by death and find thoughts of our own mortality and shiver in the chill of its breath.*

(Air candle is lighted.)

In the wan light of the stricken Sun we seek warmth to drive away the spectre of death we see.

(Fire candle is lighted.)

We feel the building breakers of depression, waves of violence, and viciousness rising within us in response to our fear of Death.

(Water candle is lighted.)

We stand beneath the Elder, its last fruit falling to the hardened ground below. In its skeletal branches are mute reminders of a tree of crucifixion, each leaf a hanging Judas. The fallen leaves bring memory of flints and shafts, bringers of death in the long ago.

(Earth candle is lighted)

HPS: *It is the Tree of Doom, the thirteenth tree, visible in the spectral light of the thirteenth Moon. It is the Death of the Year.*

The Goddess places the Death-knowledge within us.

(Touches the left palm)

It is our understanding and awareness of Her Life-in-Death that gives our expression of that knowledge form the outside world can see.

(Writes Ogham Ruis in right palm)

HP: *Thus the strokes of Ruis, the symbol of the Elder tree, mark once more the pentad of the Goddess within us: Birth, Maiden, Mother, Crone, and Protector of the Dead.*

Within this Moon is also the extra day of the year, the portal of life. Take also another symbol. From the two lands of Egypt comes a letter equal to the Elder.

(HPS draws the Egyptian "R," the mouth, in the left palm.)

HPS: *The mouth is that into which we draw our first nourishment and our breath, and from the death of the oxygen-richness of indrawn breath comes the birth of spoken thought. Once more is there promise of the Life-to-come concealed in apparent death.*

MAIDEN: *The Summons to Death has been sent. The world still mourns the passage of the Sacred King.*

The winds rise, and their voices are heard above the keening world and the tumult of the stormy seas.

Eurus echoes memories of new growth and springtime.

Notus murmurs of the brilliance and warmth of the summer Sun.

Zephyrus sings of the Cauldron of Rebirth.

Boreas whispers of Life-in-Death, the seeds within the fallen fruit.

Listen to the Winds.

(Play winds tape during meditation time, then slowly fade sound out.)

(As HP states the following, HPS walks slowly about the perimeter of the circle, allowing one white feather to fall from overhead, and drift down to each person in circle. She then returns to her position in circle.)

HP: *The winds have calmed. The sea is serene. We hear the mewling cry of the Halcyon as we enter the seven days before the Winter Solstice.*

The Halcyon lays her eggs at the waterside and takes flight across its surface. A feather drifts from her wings in passage.

In her power to allay storms is the symbol of the Goddess of calm seas. From that serenity within we face the despair, violence, and death of this Moon with the inner knowledge of Life-in-Death, secure in the rebirth to come.

(HPS begins chant: "Evoe Kali! Ecco Kronos!")

FEAST OF THE ELEMENTS:

AIR: *Thoughts of Death shall not control us, for we breathe in Life each moment.*

(Air symbol is shared.)

FIRE: *The dying Sun shall not leave us fearful of the darkness, for we are keepers of the Sacred Flame.*

(Fire symbol is shared.)

WATER: *The crashing waves of depression and violence shall not overcome us, for we remember the Sea of Life.*

(Water symbol is shared.)

EARTH: *The death of the Year shall not cause us to act in fear. With our inner knowledge of Life-in-Death we prepare for new life to come.*

(Earth element is shared around the Circle.)

DISMISSAL OF SPIRITS:
THANKS TO DEITIES:
CIRCLE IS ENDED:

Making things fit together . . .

There is Life After Ritual . . .

Now you have read and studied the tree, the Moon, or the season. You have spent time and energies identifying the mood and purpose of each, how to pronounce difficult names, and where what goes at which times. Now what? You are able to say, "I'm prepared for the ritual. I know what needs to be done." That is wonderful, but why? What is your reason for the ritual? What is your inner purpose? Is it in tune with the purpose of the ritual, whether Moon, season, or something else? What happens when the ritual is over? Once the ceremony is completed, is it just a time for "That was a nice ritual," and let it go at that? or are there longer-lasting and residual effects? Let's consider that possibility.

The items you use consistently in ritual will continue to absorb the energies and vibrations of your worship. We become so accustomed to the general effect and energy patterns that we may only notice when something seems "out of sync." For example, suppose that someone we love gives us a lovely chalice, and we replace the simple wooden one we've been using. At another time, we might find a candleholder that is just what we have wanted for our altar candles, and replace the old one. If items are not consecrated before using them in ritual, differences in energies and vibrations will be noticed. However, a subtle variance will be there for a while even after consecration. The new items will seem to be somewhat "neutral" in comparison to the rest of your ritual items. This changes as you continue to use them. The new item begins to absorb the basic vibrations with which you work. In other words, they develop a ritual "charge."

Any object you use for a specific purpose will begin to take on and hold those vibrations. This is the reason a perceptive or sensitive person is able to hold an item commonly used or worn by a particular individual and receive images and input about its source and the life of its owner or wearer.

181

As you move through the year observing Moons and solar points of the Wheel, you continue to use the items and objects in the ritual. The vibrations each one absorbs while in the sacred space relate to the energies of that rite in general and to the specific symbolism of that ritual. In addition, any inherent meaning in its nature, shape, form, or accepted symbolism will be enhanced.

Each person relates to ritual tokens in different ways. Some discard them or give them no further attention. Others retain them as ritual links. Many people will discard them periodically, when that same Moon or season comes again or at the death and rebirth of the Sun. However, most of us tend to keep the items from season to season and year to year. They become reminders of the essence of each rite, and continue to provide a hint of that stronger Higher Self which we become within that sacred circle. These items can be placed here and there around the home so that the visual impact reinforces the vibration carried from that ritual.

You may prefer to save or store the items in a special bag or container to be used as needed in future situations. At times you might choose to carry an item with you to aid in activating that quality or vibration within yourself. You could place a ritual token under your pillow to bring a greater knowledge or ability to your subconscious through the dream state.

One excellent application for later use is to set a time at year's end to cast your circle for meditation. Place within it the series of tokens which represent the year of Moons and seasons just completed. Allow a few minutes with each symbol, reviewing the meaning behind it and the events which occurred at its turn of the Wheel. Remember the seeds and goals with which you began the year. Mentally wander through its passage. Examine your actions or lack of them. Evaluate your harvest and your inner growth, which these tokens were designed to aid.

You are not limited to only passive use of these items, however. They can be utilized quite effectively as talismans or in basic spells which call on the quality or vibration they hold. Consider some of the following applications.

In personal growth during the year, certain habits or attitudes may be identified which are hindering your continued growth. The decision to do something about eliminating those undesirable traits provides an opportunity to utilize the highly charged tokens or symbol items from previous rituals. After planning your work and casting your circle, you could list those actions, habits, or attitudes on small pieces of paper. Speak aloud, designating each of the characteristics you wish to eradicate, and drop each piece of paper on the floor as a rejection of it. When you have identified them all, state your desire to eliminate them from your personal patterns, and begin sweeping them with the besom (broom) made during the Birch Moon ritual (or the Hawthorn Moon, if the brooms are used there).

The qualities of the inception Moon and new beginnings are contained within the broom from being part of that rite. Its added symbolism of sweeping clean is still stronger because of the absorbed vibrations. Continue to sweep; use a dustpan or similar object to gather the discarded characteristics for disposal. Burn them in the censer or place them in a garbage container outside your home. Then, take some time for meditation in that same circle to visualize the qualities you wish to gain, and to replace those which you have eliminated. When you have finished, close the circle in the pattern you have determined is most effective for you.

Don't overwork your magic! You cannot expect it to do the impossible, or do all the work! You must also continue with the necessary steps outside the magical circle — in the physical world — that are intended to assist you in reaching your goals. For example: when you have completed magical working to bring to you that "perfect job," do you sit by the telephone with your hand poised over it ready to respond to someone begging you to work for them? No! You still peruse the ads in the paper, send out resumes, check with the employment office, and keep interview appointments. You support and back up your magic with action.

A greater need for added communication with the Goddess may occur at another time. Here, you might wish to work with the small silvered whistle from the sixth Moon ritual. Go to a quiet, restful place and ready your mind. When you are calm and centered, with your thoughts or questions clear in your mind, blow the whistle three times to symbolically call the words of the Goddess to you, whether in the form of the winds or in meditative awareness.

One of the hazel nuts could be added to a medicine pouch or power bag. Used in this way, it becomes a talisman, invoking that symbolic wisdom as you require it or as an influence surrounding you at all times.

Suppose there is an intense dissatisfaction with a current job. There are few alternatives or directions open to you where you are, and you wish to extend your options or open more possibilities. What you seek is a position which will provide you with added opportunities for growth and advancement which are barred from you in the current situation. In essence, you want to build on the career framework already established to expand or open up a greater potential. Carefully write down the kind of job you want, the salary range you require, and the desired working atmosphere. In your cast circle, use the hinge set you have saved from the Oaken Moon. Identify your strengths and abilities that need the expansion or change in the working environment. Designate each "nail" position as one of the factors you require: salary range, working conditions, increased responsibilities, growth opportunities on and in the new job. Then "see" yourself in new surroundings, challenged but content in your everyday work environment. Once you envision that clearly, slowly open the hinge completely. You may wish to tape or pin it to a backing to maintain that position. Place it near your dresser or bathroom mirror so that it is the first thing you see on arising, or deposit it in a small bag to carry with you. It now becomes a symbol or talisman of your purpose and upcoming success, just as a door opens or expands from the framework around it to provide wider vistas.

The hinge could also be utilized in meditation to determine directions and new areas of growth and learning. It then becomes a symbol of your opening psyche and areas of developing skills. It too, can be carried with you as a talisman.

In a stressful situation, it is often difficult to remain calm and retain a workable degree of serenity. That could be a time to carry the white feather symbolizing the Halcyon from the Elder Moon. Within the vibrations stored in the feather from the ritual is the symbolic power to allay storms and a connection to the Goddess of calm seas. With a small finding available at many hobby shops or most lapidary shops, the feather can be mounted to be worn as a pendant or added to an earring or key chain. Thus, you carry a "back-up" of serenity with you. If stress levels increase suddenly and you do not have your ritual items nearby, then simply imagine the cry of the Halcyon and a feather drifting to you from her passage. After all, you were also within that circle absorbing the vibrations, just as the feather did. Reach for the serenity and power within you to allay storms and create calm seas. The feather is only a symbol of that power. The real magic is within you.

There are times, especially while working, when we must deal with the effects of situational ethics, and the unfair practices or partial truths or untruths of co-workers. It would be so easy at times to give in to the patterns and standards of behavior around us. One challenge inherent in this situation is being honest with yourself. Avoid rationalizations and excuses for your own conduct. This is an instance when you might carry a hazel nut with you, or use your lunchtime to return to the silence of the Reed Moon and examine yourself, your interactions with others, and your effect upon them.

If this is a difficulty you frequently face and have examined yourself, you may wish to take the wooden ruler you received in celebrating the autumn or harvest season. Seeing it on your desk and using it provides a constant reminder that your actions are measured by the God and Goddess. They ask a bit more than the patterns and standards of the everyday world. That may be enough loving support to allow you to take a deep breath and deal calmly with the challenge of living up to your own standards and ethics in a world which differs in its focus, and in which jealousies and resentment determine the actions of others.

This book is the result of just such a situation for me; its early research many years ago was my challenge to intolerance and lack of manners. There have been times when I simply found a quiet place and mentally re-experienced a specific ritual, because what I needed most at that moment was to freshen and reinforce what had been given me long ago in the circle.

The real challenge of this book (and of writing and conducting rituals) lay in trying to put feelings and the presence of the Old Ones into words. This is not the easiest of tasks! However, we rarely learn as much from the easy things, do we? It is from the moments that require us to dig the deepest into ourselves that we learn the most.

I have learned a great deal from something which was begun for all the wrong reasons. Universal truths are not limited. They are available to all who sincerely seek them; they are not intended to be hidden. They may, indeed, be subtle, but they are not secret! At times, they are so obvious that we do not see them. We may know a specific truth and not realize it, or we may think we know it while we, in fact, do not truly understand it.

Our real challenge lies in remembering that we do not possess the only truths, nor are we the only ones who can see them. That understanding is what we must carry into and out of ritual so that the life of the rite continues to thrive and grow within us. Thus, life after ritual not only exists, but it is richer, spiritually stronger, more rewarding, and filled with growth.

Putting it all Together

This book can be used in several ways. Obviously, it can be used as a Book of Lights and Shadows for rituals throughout the year. It could also be considered an aid in learning the Druidic tree calendar, or as a source for personal or group meditations.

My strongest desire is that it will be a reinforcement for each reader. I hope that it will support the inner beliefs which you, as a seeker, already hold, providing a framework or skeleton with which to work to build your complete belief system and patterns of working. At the same time, for the more experienced Wiccan practitioner, I would wish it to serve the purpose of augmenting the knowledge and practice you have previously established and to reaffirm what you have gained through your own efforts and studies.

I don't want much, do I? Something for Everyone? All Things to All People? Well, why not? If I hadn't thought the concepts we have discussed here had something to offer on several levels, I would not have written it; or I would have chosen some other way to write it, perhaps as a more scholarly treatise than as a description of ritual forms of worship.

The rituals are a mixture of drama, archetypal images, and inner levels of meditation. Some readers may feel they are too dramatic, and that's O.K., too. Life *can* be rather dramatic! It, too, draws upon universal truths in race or cosmic consciousness and touches something deep within us.

This series of rituals has been used as a form of worship, a teaching tool, a meditation aid, and as a means to establish channels of communication between the student and the deities or cosmic consciousness. Observing these rites has helped me to enhance the understanding of the eternal Wheel of the Year. As such, I have used some of the rituals from year to year, as they were appropriate to or focused on the needs of the circle. However, the last thing I would want them to be considered would be some form of Holy Writ, to be dogmatically repeated cycle after cycle with no change should they fail to meet the needs of the circle.

A *human person* wrote these rituals! They may well be inspired writing. I am not sure that I can always claim a complete mastery of the skills that put them together; there are times when the words or ideas flowed so smoothly from deep within that I knew a mystical Dion Fortune or Andre Norton must be hidden in some secret room of my mind and heart, penning thoughts beyond my normal talents upon the paper before me.

Yes, these rites deal with sacred subjects, but they are rendered in ordinary, everyday language. They are not worthy of binding you or enslaving your practices so as to prohibit your own growth and evolution.

Use the rituals as they are, or adapt them to the specific needs of your circle and current circumstances. Utilize the concepts presented here and add your own studies to ritualize an area of research you have found important to you. Work with the framework provided to sharpen your own ritual-writing skills. By all means, use them and enjoy them, but please do not let them become something static and unchanging, like some piece of indigestible dogma which only produces spiritual heartburn.

Nothing ever replaces that special Teacher, especially in the Craft, and this book is no exception. However, at some point, we must each realize that we are our own Teacher. We just sometimes forget the specific lessons we have set for ourselves. We become bogged down in details and minutiae of "hows" and "Am I doing this right?" Don't worry about the "proper" how-to's or whether your way of working or worship matches the "norm." There isn't one. If a method or system works for you, then use it. If it does not serve you effectively, then adapt it or use another practice.

Work with the ideas shared in this book. Try the different forms of wine blessing or Cakes and Wine to find the one or ones which work best for you. Observe your working and determine whether some of your practices are more effective in particular circumstances or certain times of the year than in others. In other words, learn your Craft!

Experiment with the elements. Without focussing in any particular direction, call each of the elementals to you. Ask them where they are most comfortable, and which quadrant point they consider home; then work that way. Set your altar to the east or the north and identify any distinctive differences in directions, or combine them and work to the northeast.

Become aware of what your practice *does*, not whether you have the approval of those around you. We are not all the same zodiac sign, the same weight or height, or the same in complexion or hair-color. None of us have precisely the same experience with the universe or reality that another person has. Thus, our worship and our working is distinctively our own and is cherished by the Lord and Lady as a unique gift of our love — to them.

For the seeker who has not found a Teacher, learn from yourself and the Lord and Lady. Think back to your earlier years. Remember the scrawled collection of squiggles and lines which you colored and handed to your mother, teacher, or grandmother, proudly informing them that it was a turtle (or whatever it was)? They may have needed your statement to know just what your picture really was, but the gift was accepted as a turtle because of your certainty of what you had drawn. It was proudly pinned to the wall or placed on the refrigerator with a magnet, and may even have been saved through the years to be remembered fondly and cherished when your own child handed you squiggles on paper and said, "See my turtle?"

As you grew older and more practiced, you learned to keep the colored marks within certain lines, making the pictures neater and more aesthetically pleasing. Still later, you mastered the skill of using circles and other geometric forms to create shapes and images that more accurately conveyed a thought or feeling.

Your learning and work in worship of the God and Goddess proceed in the same way. Your first step and your strongest tool is the clarity of your mind and heart in knowing your intent and purpose. Build slowly and solidly, with quality, on that foundation. Know that the the Lord and Lady will not just see, but will also hear the voice of the turtle in the land even as you make those first, hesitant sketches and lines of practice.

What about the reader who has training? Some of you may not yet have found what you really feel is your pathway. Others may well have completed years of training and are now responsible for teaching others. It is my hope that there is also something here for each of you. You may wish to use the rituals in this book purely for personal evaluation or to tune in to your growth patterns during the year. In the process you may find that one point or another aids you in determining your own direction. For others, the teaching aspects interwoven in these rituals may become a useful tool in training those for whom you have accepted the responsibility to teach, but who may not yet be ready to embrace your full tradition.

Whether you are a Seeker who has found no Teacher, a Teacher who still seeks to learn, or somewhere in between, use and enjoy this book and the concepts shared in it as a skeleton, fleshing it out with your own learning and joy in worshipping the Old Gods. Use it to affirm or to stretch your knowledge, to strengthen your skills and abilities, and to deepen the worship you already offer from the heart.

My thanks to the elements for their aid, to the Mother and Father of us all for their guidance, and to you, my Brothers and Sisters of our Craft, for sharing with me.

May we grow as the trees in the forest . . .

Blessed Be.

APPENDIX A

The Ogham Correspondence Charts

When I first began researching the Druidic trees, it was a matter of finding one little bit of information, then another. One reference might mention a related gemstone, while the next volume noted a bird, biblical tribe, or other correspondences. At that time, such wonderful materials as the *Celtic Tree Oracle, Fruits of the Moon Tree*, or the hard-bound *Year-and-a-Day Calendar* were not available. It was a long, slow process of garnering information in small, very incomplete segments. Finally, all the little bits and pieces went on a sheet of butcher paper on the wall, so I could see what I was missing. The Correspondences chart on the following pages is the result.

On the extreme left is the Roman letter designation which matches the Ogham tree letter. By following the data across the row, you can match the Oghmic character, its name, pronunciation, and tree with the beginning date for its month or season, the traditional and Druidic gemstones, and related Old Testament tribe as well as the color and bird assigned to that tree-letter.

References for the Judaic tribes were only found for the consonant or Moon trees/ Traditional gemstones listed are based on correlating several resources. Druidic gem correspondences were provided by a current member of an active grove. However, the quartz crystal designations as gemstones for the vowel trees or seasons are only my personal choices, and were not found or verified in any research.

I hope that this compilation will be a help to you in delving into the Sacred Trees and making your own connections.

Roman	Ogham	Name	Pronunciation	Tree	Date/Begins
A	╬	Ailm	"Ahl' em"	Silver Fir	Winter Solstice
J (II)				Mistletoe	Day after Solstice
O	╪	Onn	"Un"	Furze	Vernal Equinox
U	╪	Ura	"Oor' uh"	Heather	Summer Solstice
E	╪	Eadha	"Eh' uh"	Poplar/Aspen	Autumn Equinox
I	╪	Idho	"Ih' huh"	Yew	Day before Winter Solstice
B	⊣	Beth	"Beh"	Birch	December 24
L	⊣	Luis	"Loush" ("Loo-ish")	Rowan	January 22
N	⊣	Nion	"Knee un"	Ash	February 19
F	⊣	Fearn	"Fair un"	Alder	March 19
S	⊣	Saille	"Sahl' yeh"	Willow	April 16
H	⊢	Huath	"Hoh' uh"	Hawthorne	May 13
D	⊨	Duir	"Der" "Dur"	Oak	June 11
T	⊨	Tinne	"Chihn' uh"	Holly	July 8
C	⊨	Coll	"Cull"	Hazel	August 5
Q	⊨	Quert	"Kwert"	Wild Apple	August 5
M	⋋	Muin	"Muhn"	Vine	September 2
G	⋌	Gort	"Goert" ("Gore-it")	Ivy	September 30
Ng	⋌	Ngetal	"Nyettle"	Reed	October 28
SS (Z)	⋌	Straif	"Strauff"	Blackthorn	
R	⋌	Ruis	"Roush" ("Roo-ish)	Elder	November 25

In Old Irish an "F" is pronounced as a "V". In the Archaic forms, the "F" is spoken as a "W." A "T" before "E" or an "I" is the "Ch" (Ty) sound.

Traditional Gemstone:	Druid's Gemstone	Tribe	Color	Bird
Clear Quartz	Tourmaline	–	Piebald	Lapwing
Black Quartz	Pearl, Green Obsidian	–		Eagle
Green Quartz	Emerald/Jade	–	Dun	Cormorant
Amethyst Qtz.	Peridot and Amertine	–	Resin	Lark
Citrine Quartz	Sapphire and Swan Fluorite	–	Rufous-red	Whistling
Blue or Light Smoky Quartz	Diamond and Star Ruby	–	Very white	Eaglet
Red Sard	Imperial Topaz	Reuben	White	Pheasant
Yellow Chrysolite	Ruby	Issachar	Grey	Duck
Sea-green Beryl	Peridot and Smithsonite	Zebulon	Clear	Snipe
Fire-Garnet	Obsidian	Judah	Crimson	Gull
Blood-red Carbuncle	Sugulite,Uvulite, Peridot	Gad	Fine-colored	Hawk
Lapis Lazuli	Carnelian	Levi	Terrible-Colored	Night Crow
White Carnelian	Moonstone	Asher	Black	Wren
Yellow Cairngorm	Blue Topaz, Rose Quartz	Simeon	Dark grey	Starling
Band-Red Agate	Opal, Magnetite	Ephraim	Brown	Crane Mouse Hen
Amethyst	Amethyst	Manasseh	Variegated	Tit-mouse
Yellow Serpentine	Lepidolite, Jasper	Dan	Blue	Mute Swan
Clear Green Jasper	Green Jasper	Dinah	Glass-Green	Goose
			Bright-colored	Thrush
Dark-Green Malachite	Mother of Pearl	Naphtali	Blood-red	Rook

Coll means "life force within you." O's are rather dull unless accented. An "R" or "L" in a word adds a slight syllable.

Comparison Chart to North American and other Native Trees

Although my family could be traced back to the late 1500's in Britain, I did not live there, and had never visited the Isles. Thus, on finding an internal resonance to the concepts of the sacred trees and their mythologies, I began searching for those comparable trees which were native to the country of my birth.

This was a slow and frustrating process. Gradually, the discovery of others who were involved in the same quest developed a network resource of hard-won data. For much of the material in the chart on the next two pages, I am extremely grateful to each of my fellow "tree-finders," especially to Dr. James Lawler and all his hours of research which he willingly shared.

There are a few empty spots in the chart where a proper tree correlation could not be logically made, and those have been left blank for you to fill in as you find the corresponding trees. For such areas as Old Egypt or 70 A.D. Rome, some possibilities could not be documented, and thus were not included. However, you will find more comprehensive comparisons for the Limberlost area of Northern Indiana, Indiana in general, Northern California, Texas, the Pacific Northwest, and for South Carolina.

Tidbits of lore about the trees and other flora of our North American continent (particularly within the United States) are included following the charts. Where possible, the dominant male and dominant female trees were designated. If you have labored in the same quest, perhaps this date will be helpful. As you find missing links, I certainly hope that you will share that discovery and your reasons for making those connections.

HISTORICAL EQUIVALENTS TO DRUIDIC SACRED TREES

Moon	*Ogham*	*British*	*Rome 70 A.D.*	*Old Egypt*

Consonant Trees

Moon	*Ogham*	*British*	*Rome 70 A.D.*	*Old Egypt*
1st	Beth	Birch		Wheat
2nd	Luis	Rowan		Pomegranate
3rd	Nion	Ash	Ash	Lotus
4th	Fearn	Alder	Olive	Parsea
5th	Saille	Willow	Willow	Kadota Fig
6th	Huath	Hawthorne	Laurel	Thorn Tree
7th	Duir	Great Oak	Roman Pine	Date Palm
8th	Tinne	Holly Oak		Onion/Radish
9th	Coll	Hazel		Grapevine
	Quert	Wild Apple		
10th	Muin	Vine	Grape (Bacchus)	Royal Palm
11th	Gort	Ivy	Ivy	Taramac
12th	Ngetal	Reed	Flax	Papyrus
		(Dwarf Elm)		
	Straif	Blackthorn		
13th	Ruis	Elder		Barley

Vowel Trees

W. Solstice		Silver Fir		Lebanon Cedar
V. Equinox		Furze		Lettuce
S. Solstice		Heather		Grass
A. Equinox		White Poplar	Lombardy Poplar	Acadia
Day prior to Solstice		Yew	Cypress	Djed Pillar
Extra Day		Mistletoe	Mistletoe	Mistletoe

NORTH AMERICAN EQUIVALENTS TO DRUIDIC SACRED TREES

Ogham	British	Indiana	Limberlost	No. California
		Consonant Trees		
Beth	Birch	River Birch	River Birch	Aspen
Luis	Rowan	Red Cedar	Red Cedar	Rosewood
Nion	Ash	Redbud	Northern Ash	Ponderosa
Pine				
Fearn	Alder	Maple	Water Maple	Alder
Saille	Willow	Willow	Willow	Willow
Huath	Hawthorn	Sycamore	Sycamore/Laurel	Cottonwood
Duir	Great Door	Eastern Oak	Beech	No. Sequoia
Tinne	Holly	Black Walnut	Black Walnut	Coastal Pine
Coll	Hazel	Beech	White Oak	Western Oak
Quert	Apple	Crabapple	Crabapple	Orange
Muin	Vine	Fiveleaf	Wild Grape	Brackenfern
Gort	Ivy	Elm	Elm	Blackberry
Ngetal	Dwarf Elm	Cattail	Cattail	Horsetail
Straif	Blackthorn			
Ruis	Elder	Persimmon	Hickory	Lodgepole Pine
		Vowel Trees		
W. Solstice	Silver Fir	Locust	N. White Pine	Douglas Fir
V. Equinox	Furze	Sweetgum	Sweetgum	Silver Spruce
S. Solstice	Heather	Blackberry	Silver Poplar	Silver Fir
Day prior to				Hemlock
Solstice	Yew	Dogwood	Dogwood	Winter
Extra Day	Mistletoe	Mistletoe	Mistletoe	Mistletoe

NORTH AMERICAN EQUIVALENTS TO DRUIDIC SACRED TREES

Moon	British	Texas	Pacific NW	So. Carolina

Consonant Trees

Moon	British	Texas	Pacific NW	So. Carolina
Beth	Birch	Gum	Aspen	Palmetto
Luis	Rowan	Tex. Red Cedar	Madrone	So. Red Cedar
Nion	Ash	American Elm	Ponderosa Pine	Redbud
Fearn	Alder	Alder	Alder	So. Wh. Magnolia
Saille	Willow	Willow	Willow	Willow
Huath	Hawthorne	Cottonwood	Cottonwood	Cottonwood
Duir	Great Oak	Mesquite	Western Cedar	So. Great Oak
Tippe	Holly Oak	Ashe Jupiter	Sitka Spruce	Holly
Coll	Hazel	Pecan	Western Oak	Beech
Quert	Wild Apple	(Apple)	Apple	Cumquat
Muin	Vine	Mulberry	Brackenfern	Grape Heliotrope
Gort	Ivy	( )	Blackberry	Ivy
Ngetal	Reed	Cattail	Horsetail	Carolina Cane
Straif	Blackthorn	Blackthorn Gum		
Ruis	Elder	Myrtle	Lodgepole Pine	Loblolly Pine

Vowel Trees

Moon	British	Texas	Pacific NW	So. Carolina
W. Solstice	Silver Fir	S. Lnglf Pine	Douglas Fir	So. Yellow Pine
V. Equinox	Furze	Sycamore	Pacific Yew	So. Sweetgum
S. Solstice	Heather	Sagebrush	Scotch Broom	Span. Tree Moss
A. Equinox	White Poplar	Bl. Hickory	Silver Fir	Hickory
Day prior to Solstice	Yew	Cypress	W. Hemlock	Cypress
Extra Day	Mistletoe	Mistletoe	Mistletoe	Mistletoe

The Solar Trees — The Vowels

A - AILM - The Silver Fir (or Palm)
Day of Winter Solstice
Season of Rebirth

The Silver Fir is a female tree, the birth tree, and is stationed at the time of the Winter Solstice. It is a symbol of protection with foliage closely resembling the Yew. Sacred to Artemis, a Greek goddess who presided over childbirth, it is the principle birth tree of Northern Europe and is familiar in any nativity context. In the Orkney area of Scotland, the new mother and child are "sained" by whirling a fir-candle three times around their bed. The Silver Fir corresponds to the Palm, which is the sacred birth tree of Egypt, Phoenicia, Babylonia, and Arabia. In the Babylonian story of the Garden of Eden, the Palm is the Tree of Life.

Known as Taram (or Tamar) in Hebrew, it is the equivalent of Ishtar or Ashtaroth, forms of the White Goddess. In the form of the Palm, it is an unarmed tree. Arabians adored the Palm of Nejran as a goddess, even draping it with clothing and ornaments and using it as an ornament for women in an annual celebration. The Phoenix in many legends is born and reborn in a Palm.

Birth-tree aspects of the Palm are carried out in its growth patterns. The Sea is Universal Mother, and the Palm thrives close to it. Without the salt water for its roots, the palm is stunted. Compare its growth with the gestation for a human child and its development in the similar "sea-water" of the womb.

Boldness and fidelity are its qualities, and it is considered a good luck token to be given to departing friends.

Ailm shares its station in the year with its sister tree, the Yew. Their placement upon the day before and the day of Winter Solstice brings the birth and death aspects of the yearly cycle to full circle.

Used frequently as an ornamental tree because of the sweet fragrance of its resin, it is known in North America as the Balsam Fir. In its birth aspect, following the death symbology of the Yew, its use has come down through the years in the present-day use of Christmas trees during the mid-winter season.

Many correspondences of evergreens other than the Silver Fir bear out its character of birth and rebirth. Both Attis and Osiris, in some myths, were imprisoned in Pine trees or logs, and that log was burned a year later, thus freeing the god in rebirth. Thus, the symbolism of the pine cone in religious ceremonies as representative of resurrection. This concept may have been an original impetus to what became the Yule log. The timing of the god's imprisonment around mid-summer and his release at mid-winter also suggests the Wheel of the Year and its continuous cycle of birth, death, and rebirth.

O - ONN - The Furze or Gorse
Spring Equinox Day
Season of Spring

The Furze or Gorse is the Sun at Spring Equinox. The fires of the Sun in spring "tame" winter and promote growth. In the same way, the spring-fires which are set in the hills "subdue" or burn away the old prickles of the Furze or Gorse. This makes the new shoots edible for sheep and encourages growth of new shoots and grass, thus promoting the return of life.

The letter O is placed at the threshold of the calendar Dolmen, next to the Birch-to-Saille pillar. In the hand it belongs at the base of the forefinger, which is dedicated to Jupiter, god of shepherds. The spring gorse-fires were burned in his honor and in recognition or petition of the return of spring. In these fires, an invocation of both God and Goddess, you find their presence: "I am the blaze on every hill."

The traditional festival of Easter is named for Oestara (Ostara or Onn-nion-a), the goddess of spring, of rebirth, and the return of life to the Earth. The name comes from the combination of Onn, the Goddess, and Nion, the tree of the month in which this festival always falls, Ash month. Thus you will sometimes find references of On-niona as a separate form of the Goddess, generally the Gallic ash-grove goddess, and the religious practice in some faiths of Ash Wednesday, the anointing of one's forehead with ashes.

Dun, the color of newly ploughed fields, is the color for this season-tree. Its bird, the cormorant, also has its symbolism in behavior during this season, which became Lent. With the ban on eating meat during this time and the general lack of other suitable foods, fish became a staple of the diet, and mankind became as greedy for it as the cormorant.

Its flowers are those first pollinated and frequented by the first bees of the year, and this yellow-flowered shrub, given to a woman, is considered a good-luck gift.

The Furze or Gorse symbolizes the second petal of the Lotus- cup, Initiation, as a station on the Herculean journey.

U - URA - The Heather or Linden
Day of Summer Solstice
Season of Summer

Depending upon geographical location, the solar position of mid-summer (Summer Solstice) is represented by the Heather or the Linden (Lime tree). It is the balance of the Dance of Life. This is a time of maturity, ripeness, and fullness.

It is sacred to Isis of Egypt, Venus Erycina (a Roman and Sicilian love goddess), and to Uroica, the Gallic Heather goddess whose name combines the Oghmic Ura and *ereice*, the Greek word for Heather. Inscriptions referring to her have been found in Roman Switzerland. Garbh Ogh, an ancient, ageless giantess of legend, gathered stones to form a triple cairn for herself in which to die in the season of the blooming Heather.

Heather or Linden flowers strongly attract bees, and are valued as a source of honey unsurpassed in flavor and delicacy. The Goddess as Cybele is often pictured as the Queen Bee. It is easy to see the symbolism of the Goddess at mid-summer, when She is called "The Queen of Every Hive."

By legend, Cybele imprisoned Attis in wood at this time of year. Osiris, brother-husband of Isis, was also imprisoned in the Heather tree (or pine, depending upon the source or editor of the myth).

Heather-ale, another favorite restorative drink, is referred to in poetry as "Heather comforting the battered poplar," or "the heath gives consolation to the toil-spent folk."

The Heather is the marriage petal of the five-petalled lotus-cup. It is thus union and the strength of the god and goddess.

White Heather is a lucky charm and protection against danger. Purple Heather represents beauty in solitude and admiration. Heather ale is a popular Welsh restorative. Linden or Heather blossoms are used for brewing a delightful tea. Linden leaves present the shape of a standard playing-card heart, suitably appropriate to its association with love goddesses.

The letter *U* is placed at the base or mound beneath the middle (Saturn) finger. The similarities between Saturn and Osiris, to whom the Reed is sacred, is evident in Reed's place as the lowest consonant on that finger. On the Calendar Dolmen, U is the center of the threshold.

The color and bird symbolism of this season-tree are strongly solar. At this time, the Sun is at its highest point, and the Lark sings as it flies upward to adore the Sun. Because of the intensity of the heat at this time of year, trees may split and ooze resin, which is the color of the honey that Heather yields.

In areas of flat plains, the Linden, known as Basswood in North America, became a substitute for the Mountain Heather. However, in the House of the Forest of Lebanon, the Cedar of its pillars and beams was sacred to Astarte or Anatha. This temple was dedicated to the love and battle goddess of Mount Lebanon. Anatha has long been considered, and cave inscriptions have been found which identify her as, the wife of Jehovah. Cedar symbolized the letter *U* in that geographic area, where Heather was the Western European equivalent.

The Heather is passionate in nature, red, and is associated with mountains and bees. In mid-summer, the males swarm to the Goddess as the Queen Bee. The joyful and voluntary self-castration of the priests of Cybele reflected the emasculation of the drone in the nuptial act. For this reason, the white Heather was also considered a protection against acts of passion.

Mount Eryx in Sicily is famed for the hero-shrine established there by the nymphs of Erycina to honor Butes, the bee-master and son of Boreas, the North Wind.

E - EADHA - The Aspen or White Poplar
Autumn Equinox Day
Season of Harvest

Autumn Equinox is the station for these trees. They symbolize the magic of joy and the aging of the year. Where the Fir is hope in divinatory use, the Black Poplar is the loss of home and hope. It is a funereal tree sacred to Mother Earth. However, the White Poplar is symbolic of resurrection, along with the Alder and the Cypress, and is a symbol of hope.

Golden headdresses of Aspen leaves have been found in burial excavations dated to 3000 B.C.E. in Mesopotamia.

Rufous-red is the color for this season-tree. This is the color of bracken and the neck of the whistling swan, the bird sacred to this tree and season. The swan and her young now prepare for flight to follow the Sun's warmth.

Hercules traveled to the springs of Ister to bring the White Poplar back to Olympia. It had been held by servants of Apollo, the Hyperboreans.

Amber is sacred to Apollo. When the sun-god Phaethon died, his sisters wept. They were transformed into poplars and their tears into amber.

Symbolic of Hercules having conquered death, the Aspen is the measuring-rod used by coffin-makers. Even in the preparation for burial the tree is the symbol of resurrection. The Styx river, long a symbol of the passages of Death, flows through a valley filled with White Poplar. Thus, at the end of life is the presence of the Goddess as a "shield for every head."

The pith of the White Poplar is star-shaped. The lustrous green of the upper leaves contrasts with its silver undersides. After his triumph in killing the giant Cacus, Hercules is said to have bound his head with Poplar. The radiant heat he gave out is, by legend, the reason for the characteristic whitened or silvered underside of the leaves. The five-pointed leaf of the Poplar is sacred to the White Goddess. Other trees, such as the silver-leaf Maple, share the qualities of five-pointed leaves and a silvered underside. Trees of those qualities are also harbingers of rain, as the leaves will turn the silvered side upward when rain is forthcoming (even with perfectly clear skies and no other apparent atmospheric indicators of rain).

Poplars flourish beside rivers, on marshes, and other watery areas. With that preference for growth near water, it is a preferred food source for the beaver, which uses Poplar trunks and branches in the construction of its dams and houses.

Perhaps its affinity for water is part of its tendency to be a poor fuel-tree. That water-density held within it may also be part of its value and endurance as a shield. It is known as the Shield-Makers' tree.

The Aspen or White Poplar is related to the North American Cottonwood. The Cottonwood's leaves flutter with the lightest breeze and are in constant motion. The French call these trees "trembles," and they are known as a symbol of lamentation and fear.

As a prophylactic against all forms of leprosy, the White Poplar seems to be effective.

In the hand, the letter *E* is placed on the mound beneath the ring finger. It is the fourth vowel tree, placed next to the last on the right of the threshold on the Calendar Dolmen.

I - IDHO - The Yew
Day before Winter Solstice
Season of Death

Stationed on the day before Winter Solstice, the longest night of the year, the Yew is the death tree throughout Europe. Even Shakespeare recognized its sacredness to Hecate by referring to the contents of her cauldron as " . . . slips of Yew, silver'd in the Moon's eclipse. . . " in *Macbeth*.

Its death references abound. Bulls sacrificed to Hecate in Rome were wreathed in Yew. In Ireland, as wine barrels are made from Yew staves, it is considered the coffin of the vine. The cut foliage is deadly to people and animals, and the bark is also poisonous.

Even its prime use in bow-making accents her character of deadliness. The Yew is legendary for its use in making deadly bows and dagger handles. The compound used by the ancient Irish to poison their weapons is said to be of Yew-berry, hellebore, and devil's bit. The Latin *taxus* (Yew) is connected with *toxon*, which is Greek for bow, and with *toxicon*, Greek for the poison for arrows.

The timber of the Yew was also used for household vessels and breastplates, as well as for burning as Yew-logs in the wintertime.

Differences existed between the British and Irish Yew. In Ireland, the branches grew straight up rather than horizontally, and the tree was cone-shaped. As one of the Five Magical Trees of Ireland, the Tree of Ross was referred to as "a firm, straight deity." Another Yew was considered the "renown of Banbha" as the death aspect of the Irish triple Goddess. The practice of an Irish king wearing a wheel-shaped brooch, entailed to his successor, was a reflection of "The Spell of Knowledge, and the King's Wheel." This is a reference to the death-letter, the I, a reminder of the king's destiny, and the full circle of the wheel of existence.

On a tin scroll in a bronze urn on Mount Ithome were secret mysteries of the Great Goddess. The urn had a Yew on one side and the Myrtle, Greek equivalent of the death consonant R (Elder), on the other.

Two lovers, Naoise and Deirdre, were buried on either side of Armagh Cathedral. Yew stakes were driven through the corpses to keep them apart. However, the stakes rooted and grew into Yew trees that ultimately merged the tops of their branches over the cathedral. Legends of Brittany suggest that Yew trees planted in a church-yard burial ground will spread a root to the mouth of each corpse.

In the time of Gwion, two fruit trees — the Yew and the Rowan — were considered dower-trees which grew in the churchyard. Yew berries fell at the porch of the church, where the marriage would be celebrated, and were prized for their sticky-sweetness.

The eaglet is associated with Idha, the day before Winter Solstice. Like Death, its maw is insatiable, and the bones in the nest are white like the snow on its cliff-ledge. Thus the connection of white as its color. A full-uddered she-goat is also appropriate to this season, as this is the time when first kids are dropped. Amalthea, mother of the horned Dionysus, is symbolized by the she-goat.

Mercury, assigned to the little finger, is Conductor of Dead Souls to Hecate (or Maia), the death-goddess. Idho is placed at the base of this finger. The death-letter I and the Yew are placed at the extreme right of the threshold of the Calendar Dolmen at the base of the autumn pillar.

Just as its day of the year is that of the longest night, the shadow of the Yew is denser than that of any other tree. It is the latest to reach full maturity, sharing that characteristic with the Oak, but it lives still longer than the Oak. When its wood is seasoned and polished, it has extended powers of endurance and resistance to decay and corruption.

As a tree of faith and resurrection, it is appropriate that in Old England it was considered the Witches' tree. It is the death-letter by which the Wheel of the Year is completed. It stands next to the Silver Fir; together they are the longest night and lengthening light, death and birth. Their foliage is so close as to be identical, making it difficult to forget the connection of labor to both death and birth.

Silver is the metal for the Fir, and it is to lead as the Fir is to the Yew.

The Fir and silver are the Moon and are connected to Birth. Lead and the Yew are Saturn, related to Death. Yet both metals are extracted from the same ore. This aspect of Life-in-Death and Death-in-Life are the substance of the Goddess' statement for this season: "I am the tomb to every hope."

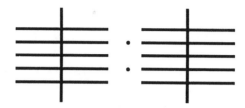

II - (Y) - The Mistletoe
Day after Winter Solstice
Extra Day — Day of Liberation

The Mistletoe is a primary phallic symbol central to many forms of authority. Among the Druids, the ceremony of cutting the Mistletoe from the Oak represented the new King emasculating the old King. This was done with a golden sickle shaped like a crescent. Within the single item used to harvest the Mistletoe is the color of the Sun and the shape of the Moon, a combination which symbolizes the strongest procreative principle, male and female conjoined.

In Viking mythology, the Mistletoe was considered too young to promise not to harm the beloved son of the Goddess and, thus, was the only living, growing thing not to so promise. Loki used that fact to fashion the death of Balder, the Sun-god.

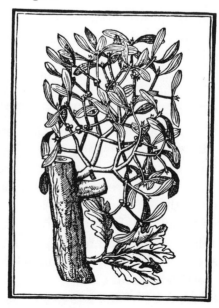

Remains of the Mistletoe have been found in tree coffins dated to the Bronze Age. Gallic Mistletoe rituals featured sacred bulls the color of its berries.

The serpent, rock dove, and Mistletoe — all sexual symbols — were sacred to and symbolized Hercules and his Egyptian equivalent, Shu.

The thirteenth part of Osiris' body, his phallus, is sometimes symbolized by the Mistletoe. Part of the connection is because of the similarity in viscosity between the Mistletoe berries and sperm. In absence of the phallus, Isis fashioned one of wood and begot Horus to avenge his father.

Consistent with the successor supplanting the old ruler, Aeneas, son of Anchises, carried a bough of the Mistletoe when he went to the underworld to cross-examine his father.

In many cultures world-wide you will find evidence of mid-summer rites featuring the binding of the king or ruler in a five-fold bond of the wrists, ankles, and neck. For some of these the bond is a single uniting of those five points. In others the Sun-King is bound on a Sun-Wheel at the five points appropriate to those body parts. With a few of those examples the ruler is impaled on a stake of Mistletoe.

Although slow growing, the wood of the Mistletoe is tough and hard. If left undisturbed long enough, it will grow to a size and length to make spears, if desired. No other tree leafs fresh in the winter. The green of its leaves, white of its berries, and gold of its flowers are echoed in the pillars and lintel of the Temple at Tyre. It is also the only one of the Druidic trees which remains the same throughout the world. It grows, as Mistletoe, on all continents except Antarctica.

Poetic expressions refer to the Mistletoe as "a tree that is not a tree," which is simultaneously low and lofty. This is most appropriate to the tree for a "Day that is not a Day." It is not a tree of itself, but it grows in a symbiotic relationship with another tree, taking its nourishment from that tree. It is normally found on the Oak, which is the emblem of the Sun-King's height and strength. The Mistletoe thus symbolically becomes the phallus of the Sun-King.

It is also referred to in many passages of literature. Debates still rage over whether Robert Frost refers to the common horsemint or the Mistletoe as the All-Heal or Heal-All in his verses. No formal scientific evidence exists of beneficial or medicinal qualities; however, there are homeopathic and holistic treatments utilizing the Mistletoe.

Correspondences for the Mistletoe and the Extra Day of the Year are: the Gryphon-Eagle, an immortal creature; the gem, amber; and the herb hyssop. It is assigned to the tribe of Benjamin, which symbolized the son on the right hand and ruler of the southern lands.

With some forms of the Ogham the Mistletoe (II or Y) completes a 72-stroke alphabet. This is especially magical, as seventy-two is the product of 9 (lunar wisdom) and 8 (solar increase), which is the true basis of the magical workings of most of the world religions.

The extra day of the year is preceded by the Silver Fir, as a tree of Rebirth, and is followed the next day by the beginning of Birch Month, tree of Inception, to begin the Solar Year once more.

In some traditions, the Mistletoe is sought out at mid-summer and is cut to fall free into a consecrated cloth. Not touched by the hands, it is left in that holy covering until autumn. At that time the cloth is opened. The mid-summer-sacrificed Mistletoe is now a golden bough.

Notes on the Lunar Trees

BETH - B - The Birch
1st Lunar Month
Bird: Pheasant
Color: White
Gemstone: Red Sard

The self-propagating Birch is the first tree of the winter season. This is the coldest season in northern climates. The atmosphere at this time compares to the dark of the Moon, even though the light of the Sun is waxing. This is a time of sleep in preparation for rebirth. The Sun has been reborn, but it takes time for its warmth to stir everything to life again. Despite the solar rebirth, it is a time of knowing and of death.

Birch is a healer of skin and joint ills. By tradition, a gift of a sprig of Birch to a love was encouragement. It indicated "You may begin."

LUIS - R - The Rowan
2nd Lunar Month
Bird: Duck
Color: Red
Gemstone: Yellow Chrysolite

Often found near stone circles, the Rowan (Mountain Ash, Quicken, or Quickbeam) is considered oracular. It is the tree of quickening, symbolizing the rebirthing of the year as life begins to respond to the Sun's warmth.

The Gaelic Fire Festival, commonly called Candlemas, occurs in this Moon month. This festival is a celebration for Brigit, a quickening Muse form of the Triple Goddess. In some areas, because Candlemas was midway between Winter Solstice and spring, the old fire would be put out, and the fire for the new year would be kindled and blessed. Some branches of Wicca traditionally consider this festival and Rowan Moon the best time for initiations. In fact, it is also called the Witch Tree.

The growths which form on the Rowan tree were considered to hold all knowledge; thus, the wattles were valued and the tree considered oracular. Certain Roman officers — lictors — carried Rowan rods as a symbol of their authority, as did various other officials of the time.

The healing of the Rowan is to sustain and extend life, a quality attributed to the eating of its berries as well.

NION - N - The Ash
3rd Lunar Month
Bird: Snipe
Color: Half Clear/Half Deep-Blue
Gemstone: Sea-Green Beryl

The god-form Woden (Wotan, Odin, Gwydion) is said to have used the Ash as his steed, taking it from the Norns (a form of the Triple Goddess), who dispensed justice beneath its branches. In Scandinavian mythology the enchanted Ash, Ygdrasill, is the universe. Its roots and branches extend throughout. Wotan in Mayan/Aztec myth is also connected to a great tree.

The runic alphabet is said to have formed itself of Ash-twigs and been revealed to Odin after he hung on the Ash tree for three days and nights. Some controversy is developing, however, over whether that Great Tree of the Universe was Ash or Yew. The hallucinogenic qualities of the Yew lead many scholars today to lean toward Odin's tree as actually having been a Yew.

The ash-spirits or Meliai are supposed to have sprung from the blood of Uranus when Cronos castrated him.

In Ireland three of the Five Magic Trees (Tree of Tortu, Tree of Dathi, and Branching Tree of Usnech) were Ash. Their fall in 665 C.E. is said to symbolize the triumph over Paganism by Christian faiths.

Still standing at Killura in the 19th century was a descendant of the Sacred Tree of Creevna, an Ash. Its wood was used as a charm against drowning. This can be easily understood because it was a tree sacred to Poseidon, god of the sea. Many emigrants to America brought it with them.

Its place on the hand Ogham is on the tip of the middle or Saturn finger. The Ash is an oracular tree, which is common to all finger-tip trees. It is on the spring pillar of the Calendar Dolmen. If your preference is for the Beth-Luis-Fearn-Saille-Nion sequence, then you would place the Ash at the tip of the little finger.

The Ash is versatile in its uses. The Druidic wand with spiral decoration was made of Ash. Passing a naked child through cleft pollard ashes before sunrise was considered a cure for rupture. In ancient Ireland and Wales its wood was used to form coracle-slats and oars as well as rods for controlling horses. It was used in making king's thrones, and for the shafts of weapons and spears. It was considered the best wood for fire whether it was green or seasoned. Used in rain-making ceremonies, the Ash is said to court the lightning. It is associated with thunderstorms and lambing. In Chinese legend, eggs will balance on end only at this time of year.

The staff or stake of a Witch's besom is still composed of Ash. The Birch twigs expel evil spirits and entangle them. The Ash stake is proof against drowning, and the osier or Willow bindings are in honor of Hecate.

The shade of the Ash is so dense that it is "cruel" to whatever might grow in its shade, restricting the sunlight available to that growth. In comparison, the Alder is considered to be beneficial in its shade. The cruelty continues, in that the roots of the Ash will strangle other forest trees. It is a tree of the power resident in water or of sea-power. Yggr, Woden's other name, relates to the Greek word *hygra* or sea. This Moon month is a very wet one known for its floods. It also is a time when the day has not yet become longer than the evening, and it is considered to still be under the tutelage or influence of Night.

The Ash is sacred to Wednesday. Gods of mercurial nature belong with this tree. Its statement is "I am a Wind on the Sea." This is the month when the wind whirls as a snipe, and the wind is colorless. Thus, the bird Ogham is given as the snipe, and its color is clear. Spring Equinox occurs in the Ash Moon month.

Ash, the watery, emotional Moon, states the healing secret, "From the viper's poison comes the tonic of life." Honestly working with the emotional turmoil of this Moon to learn your inner self can result in a more effective knowledge of and stronger expression of that self.

FEARN - F - The Alder
4th Lunar Month
Birds: Crow and Gull
Colors: Crimson, Green-Brown,
Royal Purple
Gemstone: Fire-Garnet

The Alder is associated with fire and the power to reduce water. It is a symbol of resurrection, seen in the spiral setting of its buds. To the Celts, it is the faeries' tree. Valued for its excellent dyes, the Alder produces a red dye from the bark, green from its flowers, and brown from its twigs, respectively signifying Fire, Water, and Earth. When it is felled, it bleeds red.

Minstrels and Muses prize the wood for use in whistles and pipes. The healing quality of the Alder deals with doubt.

This time frame celebrates the return of the Kore (Persephone) from Hades in reunion with her mother, Demeter. This is a time to celebrate the connection and tie between women and the continuity of Mothers and Daughters, the life-force which is all-pervading in Nature.

SAILLE - S - The Willow
5th Lunar Month
Bird: Hawk
Color: Haze
Gemstone: Blood-Red Carbuncle

The fifth tree month of the Ogham consonants is sacred to Minerva, inventor of numbers, and to the Roman Moon Goddess of Wisdom. Words such as "Witch, "wicker," and "wicked" are all said to have derived from Willow. "Helice" in Greek, the Willow, gives her name to the Helicon, where the Nine Muses reside.

Beltane (Beltaine, Belteine), the second cross-quarterly festival day, occurs in the Saille month. It is sacred to Sappho, the poet, Fairy Queen Brigid, and the goddess Dana. Midway between Equinox and Summer Solstice, it celebrates the full blossoming of the spring. At May Eve, the goddess is one of Love and Death such as Freya, Frigg, Holda, Held, Hilde, Goda, and Ostara. Traditionally, this celebration was an orgiastic revel which celebrated the Maiden's coming of age and the rebirth of flowers and the fertility of the Earth.

A rejected lover would wear willow in his hat as a charm against the Moon Goddess's jealousy. Fevers and headaches are the healing concerns of the Willow.

UATH (HUATH) - H - The Hawthorn
6th Lunar Month
Bird: Nightcrow
Color: Deepest Black
Gemstone: Lapis Lazuli

The Hawthorn tree (Whitethorn, May) is a tree of enforced chastity. In this Moon month in ancient Britain and Greece, old clothes were worn, the temples were cleaned in preparation (both psychically and physically) for the mid-summer celebrations, and sexual abstinence was observed.

Modern medicine has found support for this practice. In examination of birth patterns, it seems that children conceived in this time frame are usually born during February. Statistics reveal also that there are more children born in this time frame who have disabilities or mental difficulties. That is, more deviance from the norm of the bell curve. Unless you wanted a defective child or a genius, it might be best to avoid the possibility. This might, at times, be more difficult to accomplish, as the Hawthorn is said to exude the strong scent of female sexuality.

Cardea (Roman), or the Greek Maia, cast spells with the Hawthorn, and was usually appeased in some form at marriages. This was especially true if the marriage occurred during the May month (month of the May tree or Hawthorn, not the calendar month of May), as this goddess opposed such unions. Guardian of hinges, she has the power to open what is closed away and conceal what is open. She looks both forward or backward in Time. Benefactress of craftspeople, she lives in a starry castle at the hinge of the universe behind the North Wind. She is Keeper of the Four Winds.

Hawthorn healing relates to balancing the blood, nerves, and spirit.

DUIR - D - The Door Oak
7th Lunar Month
Bird: Wren
Color: Black
Gemstone: White Carnelian

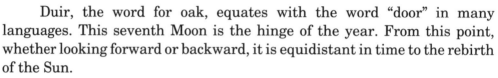

Duir, the word for oak, equates with the word "door" in many languages. This seventh Moon is the hinge of the year. From this point, whether looking forward or backward, it is equidistant in time to the rebirth of the Sun.

The Oak is one of the slowest trees to reach full maturity, but it is a tree of endurance and triumph with strong, tough wood. It is exceeded in life endurance only by the yew, its counterpart at the end/beginning of the solar year. Its root system reaches as deeply into the Earth as its topmost branches thrust into the sky. It is emblematic of the Universal Law which rules, "As Above, So Below."

Summer Solstice occurs in the month of the Oak Moon, bringing the shortest night and longest day. It is celebrated with blazes dedicated to those goddesses who would be considered Fire Queens of Love, such as Hertha, Arianrhod, Artemis, Rhea, Calliste. It marks the beginning of summer even though it is often referred to as mid-summer because of the increasing heat of the season. The promise of Spring is fulfilled in this season.

This is a Moon for the Goddess of the Mill, at the axle of the world, turning without motion. Ursa Major or Ursa Minor (the Great and Little She-Bears in astronomy) turn this mill and are sacred to Artemis, Calliste, Cardea, Eurynome, and Rhea.

The Oak is the glorious Sun-King at his maturity and is the celestial tree for Druidic Celts. The Oak and its companion, the Mistletoe, were an integral part of their ceremonies.

Its fruit, the acorn, was a primary food source for Nordic tribes and was, in itself, a symbol of fruitfulness and immortality.

According to some traditions, the Oak was the tree for the Yule log, not the Yew. By tradition, it must be found — not cut. The increased interest in its parasite, the Mistletoe, at the Winter season and as the tree for the Extra Day of the Year is intriguing. The Oak is life, endurance, strength; and the Mistletoe is beautiful but poisonous. Thus, the combination is that of Life and Death, Death and Life.

Cleansing and strengthening are the Oak's healing qualities.

TINNE - T - The Holly (or Scarlet Oak)
8th Lunar Month
Bird: Starling
Color: Green-Grey
Gemstone: Yellow Cairngorm

The eighth Moon month is the month of the barley harvest. Eight is the number of increase and was one of the preferred numbers of the Pythagoreans. The Celtic word for sacred tree is Tinne. Holly means "holy." The eighth consonant tree, flowering in July, is a symbol of foresight and defense, with a message of "I dare not approach." It was often used for making chariot shafts.

An evergreen oak, twin to the seventh Moon's Oak, the Holly was a tree which the Druids felt always had the Sun. Winter refuges of evergreen were placed inside buildings for the woodland spirits. The sacred Druidic oak ruled the waxing year, and the evergreen scarlet oak ruled the waning year.

Thunder gods, such as Tina Etruscan (Goidelic), armed with a triple thunderbolt, and Tannus (Gaulish), relate to the Scarlet Oak, and it was sacred to them (as can be seen in the similarities in the names). An evergreen Oak grove near Corinth was considered sacred to the Furies.

For the Romans the Holly was connected to the Saturnalia and was a token of good will and good wishes. It was also the tree of the ass-god, whereas the mid-summer oak was that of the wild-ox, its twin.

Some historians have pondered the connections between the ass-god cults existing in Jerusalem and the entry of Jesus, riding an ass. It is an intriguing consideration, as the ass-god and the evergreen oak have always killed their twins, the wild-ox and the mid-summer oak. It does make one wonder.

Native Americans considered and planted Holly around dwellings as a protection. In some tribes a sprig was worn during childbirth for easing the pain and invoking the health of the child to come.

The "Terebinth" of the Christian Bible refers to the oak, and scarlet terebinth refers to the Holly or Kerm Oak. Its leaves are prickly, and it nourishes a scarlet insect called the kerm. The royal scarlet dye, which resembles the insect's color, was made by the ancients from the Holly berry along with an aphrodisiac elixir.

Cerridwen, clad in such a scarlet, sits between the Oak and the Holly (between the Oak King and the Holly King). She has given birth to and accepted one of them as lover. In the passage of the year, She sees Her lover killed by his brother; is loved by the Holly King; and gives birth to Her Love again at Yule. In this eternal sequence it is easy to see the immortal Green Knight (the mid-summer Oak) as a giant with a Holly-bush club (the Tanist, or Holly King who must kill his other self in order to be reborn). The last twenty-four hours of the old year are ruled over by the Holly King.

Looking honestly at the events and history, we must place John the Baptist as the Oak King and Jesus, called the Christ, as the Holly King. Thus, modern religious practices worship the Lord of Death, rather than the Lord of Life, despite inference to the contrary. In this light it is easy to see why Holly and Ivy have come to be accepted as suitable for church decoration at the Christmas season, and the Mistletoe is forbidden as pagan.

However, the Holly and Ivy rivalry is not the battle between the tree of murder and resurrection but a battle of the sexes. For more on this competition see the section on Ivy. The Holly Boy was associated with the Saturnalia in ancient Italy, as the Holly was Saturn's club. A dark man, as representative of Saturn, must be the first to step over the threshold on Yule morning. To insure this, women were kept out of the way, giving impetus to the conflict or competition of the Ivy Girl and Holly Boy.

In this Moon Month is the celebration of August Eve, the first harvest. It is the third cross-quarterly celebration of the year, called Lammas, Lugh-mas, or Lughnasad. The American Indian Corn Mothers are honored at this time in a celebration of Habondia, the Goddess of Plenty. Kore and Ceres are also honored at this time. While it is an early harvest rite, it is also a day of mourning for dead loved ones.

The Spear month, month of the Tanist, influenced ancient letters — the bardic T was shaped like a barbed spear. The Holly Moon is a warrior's Moon. Thus the dark-grey of iron, the warrior's metal, is appropriate. The Starling as the Bird Ogham symbol refers to its practice as an army of birds which turn or move as one with no apparent signal or communication. The message of the Starling in this Moon is that battles are won by concerted, joint efforts, not by individual acts and broken unity.

In the hand, the Holly is the first digit of the middle or Saturn finger, beneath the finger-tip tree, the Ash. On the calendar Dolmen, it is placed on the lintel near the autumn pillar.

As one of the seven Chieftain trees, Holly would seem to say, "I am a battle-raging spear"; "I fled as a spear-head of woe to such as wish for woe";

or "I embolden the spearmen."

The Holly approaches healing from the preventative and protective viewpoint.

COLL - C - The Nut-Hazel
9th Lunar Month
Bird: Crane
Color: Brown
Gemstone: Banded Red Agate

Although the Hazel is assigned as the tree for the ninth Moon month, there are actually two trees which share that time frame: the Hazel and the Wild Apple. This is the nutting season, and the Hazel nut represents concentrated wisdom. All knowledge of the arts and sciences were given to the nine Hazels which grew near Connla's Well near Tipperary. A salmon swimming in the well fed on the nuts and gained a bright spot on its body with each nut it ate. These trees of the poetic art produced beauty (flowers) and wisdom (fruit) at the same time. Eating of the nuts from those trees conferred all knowledge and wisdom to the one who ate them. Thus, the spotted salmon, by having eaten the Hazel nuts, contained and were symbols of all knowledge. This is especially significant in that the Hazel bears fruit in its ninth year. It is the tree of white magic and healing.

In the tale of Taliesin or Finn, son of a Chief Druid's daughter, he was instructed by the Druid to cook him a salmon but was forbidden to taste it. However, in cooking it, he burned his thumb. When he put the thumb in his mouth, he was inspired with knowledge and the arts because the salmon had fed on the Hazel nuts. Other variations of the tale may lead on into the love-chase scenario with the Goddess.

By tradition, if a lover is given a piece of Hazel, his message is to " . . . be wise and desist." He would prefer the sprig of Birch, which suggests that he may begin courting.

Nine is a number of completion and the number of the Moon. It is a number sacred to the Muses, who were daughters of Zeus, king of the gods and Mnemosyne, goddess of memory. They were: Calliope — epic poetry; Clio — history; Urania — astronomy; Erato — love poetry; Euterpe — lyric poetry; Melpomene — tragedy; Polyhymnia — sacred song; Terpsichore — dance; and Thalia — comedy.

Many feel that the Y-shaped divining rod is best effective if it is made from the fork of a Hazel branch. In seventeenth- century England the Hazel divining rod was used to find those guilty of murder or theft and to seek for water or treasure. Irish heralds carried white Hazel wands. The value of time and patience is the healing of the Hazel.

The Ancient Dripping Hazel was a tree of wisdom to be put to destructive uses. It was without leaves and was the resting place for vultures and ravens, birds of divination. The sap it dripped was poisonous.

MUIN - M - The Vine
10th Lunar Month
Animal: Snake and Tit–Mouse
Color: Variegated
Gemstone: Amethyst

The tenth tree, the Vine, is at once a symbol of the simplicity of joy, the heights of exhilaration, and the dregs of wrath. This is the vintage season. Symbolic of peace and abundance as well as of fortune and enduring strength, the bramble or wild-growing vine governs inspiration, imagination, poetry, and imagery. The essence of all contained within the Vine is retained, in strength, in her wine. It is sacred to Dionysus, Osiris, and Bacchus, and its five-pointed leaves are sacred to the White Goddess.

It is associated with the elm, as those trees were used in the British Isles to support the young vines.

The lowest joint on the thumb is the placement for the vine in the Hand Ogham. On the Calendar Dolmen, it falls on the autumn pillar on the right.

Celtic countries observed a taboo against eating the blackberries (bramble or wild-vine) at certain times of the year. However, the reasons vary significantly. The only reason given in Brittany is "because of the fairies . . ." The berries are considered poisonous in the northern part of Wales. In Devonshire the taboo is only observed from October onward, as they supposedly become inhabited by the devil at that time. In Majorca the bramble berries represent the blood of Christ, and its vine was selected for his crown of thorns.

The Autumnal Equinox is celebrated in the tenth lunar month, marking the point in the Wheel of the Year where the nights begin to grow longer once again. The waning of the Sun's light becomes more noticeable after this celebration, and auroras may be more frequent.

This is the harvest season, sacred to Demeter, goddess of the harvest. The richness of the harvest, the lightened atmosphere after the heat of the summer, and the hint of crispness to come with the cold of winter, fill this season.

In its expression, the Vine says, "I am a Hill of Poetry." Tonic healing is related to the Vine.

GORT - G - The Ivy
11thLunar Month
Bird: Mute Swan
Color: Blue
Gemstone: Yellow Serpentine

The Vine and the Ivy are the only sacred trees which grow in a spiral. That growth is similar to chromosomic patterns, which are doubly helical. They are both trees of resurrection. The Ivy is sacred to Osiris and is the nest of the gold crest wren, Saturn's bird. The leaves used for the Poet Laureate crown are those of the Ivy, as they were for the wreath of Bacchus.

Eternal friendship, attachment, and fidelity are qualities of the Ivy. The Osirian Ivy (Hedera Helix), along with the vine, bramble, fig, plane tree, briar-rose, primrose, periwinkle, cinquefoil, and some poplar leaves, are all five-pointed and are therefore sacred to the White Goddess.

Dionysus wreathed everything with Ivy when he changed the pirates' masts into serpents, made dolphins of the sailors, and became a lion.

Bassarids, a pack of delirious women who had drunk the Ivy and toadstool sacred to Dionysus, tore Orpheus to pieces as a result of Ariadne's anger. However, his head continued to predict and prophesy.

Ariadne's wreaths were spiraled with the yellow-berried Ivy in honor of the autumn Dionysus. At these October Bacchanal revels in Thessaly and Thrace the Bassarids wore roebucks tattooed above the elbows on the right arm.

In all probability they had drunk a spruce-ale laced with Ivy. The Ivy leaves, when chewed, would also have a toxic effect. However, the muscular strength needed to be able to tear bodies such as Orpheus's would have had to come from the amanita muscaria, the spotted toadstool with white spots. This is probable, as the Mysterion, the fall festival of Dionysus, related strongly to the uprising of the toadstools; drinks including those mushrooms were considered suitable food — ambrosia — for the gods.

The amanita muscaria featured in such brews grows under a Birch in areas north of Thrace and in Celtic countries, but is found beneath a fir or pine south of Greece and Palestine to the equator. Its color changes as well from scarlet in the north to fox-colored in the south.

In England, many taverns boast a sign of the Ivy-bush, which is a traditional indication of a tavern. At Trinity College they still brew Ivy-ale, a very intoxicating drink from medieval times.

The last farmer to complete his harvest was given an Osirian Ivy-bound harvest sheaf. It was called the Harvest Bride, Ivy Girl, and Harvest May. Until the next year, he held that sheaf to be an ill-luck omen or penalty. Because of this, a shrewish wife, a carline, and the Harvest Bride were compared to Ivy, due to the tendency of the plant to strangle the trees on which it grows.

Another association with Ivy Girl relates to the competition between the women and men on Yule morning. By tradition the first foot over the threshold had to be the Holly Boy, Saturn's representative. Much effort was expended to keep women out of the way until that was accomplished.

The Ivy month is symbolized by the boar. Mythology provides several examples: Disguised as a boar, Set killed Osiris; Finn McCool murdered Diarmuid, who was lover to Grainne; Apollo, as a boar, slew Adonis (Tammuz) over Aphrodite. Artemis' lover Ancaeus and Zeus of Crete were also murdered by a boar.

Autumn, the beginning of the death of the year, starts in the month before the boar, which is a symbol of that same death. The month of the Ivy is a time of revelry and the boar-hunting season.

Halomas (Samhain, Hallows, Hallowe'en), the final cross-quarterly festival of the year, occurs in Ivy month. At this time the veil between the worlds of Man and Spirit are the thinnest, and contact can be made with those you love who have gone on in transition. This is a festival which honors the third face of the Goddess, the destroyer or Crone. Wisdom and protection are the keywords for this celebration, which is appropriate to the New Year. Hecate is the goddess most recognized at this time. In the Orient, this is considered a time of ancestral worship. It is a good idea, when considering this festival as oriented to death, to remember that it is at this time that animals were slaughtered to meet the food needs of the winter.

The Whistling Swan of autumn precedes the Mute Swan in its migratory flight. Thus, the Mute Swan is the Bird Ogham for the Ivy month. As autumn begins, the atmosphere seems to thicken with the coming season, fires burn away excess growth, and there is the promise of rains to come. Therefore, the blue of that haze or veil to the sight becomes the color for Ivy Moon.

The Ivy letter is next to the top on the autumn pillar of the Calendar Dolmen. Its place in the hand is on the second phalange of the forefinger.

In expression the Ivy says: "I am a Boar (for valor); I am a ruthless Boar; I fled as a bristly boar seen in a ravine; I rove the hills like a ravening Boar; I am a fierce boar, with powers of chieftain-like valor."

Ivy's message is: "I die where I cling." The Ivy heals by calming and regulating the nerves.

NGETAL - Ng - The Reed
12th Lunar Month
Birds: Owl and Goose
Color: Green
Gemstone: Clear Green Jasper

The Reed is also known as the Water-Elder, Whitten, or Rose-petal. It is found in a wide variety of forms and has as many uses as it has appearances. It is used for making arrows and in herbal remedies to heal the wounds of an arrow.

It is a symbol of music and is utilized and of great value in making woodwind instruments such as bagpipes and flutes. It is sacred, of course, to Pan for the sake of his Pan-pipes. At this time of the year villagers rethatched their homes to assure security through the winter ahead. New couples considered their home established when the roof thatching was complete.

The Reed was a much-used tool by weavers, as it aided in separating threads and beating fibers in preparation for spinning.

The ills of over-indulgence are healed by the Reed.

RUIS - R - The Elder
13th Lunar Month
Bird: Rook
Color: Blood-Red
Gemstone: Dark Green Malachite

The Elder is another water-side tree which has become associated with Witches. Rather than seeing the association as simply that of a death tree, consider the continued cycle that the Witches see: Life-in-Death and Death-in-Life, a never-ending cycle.

The blossoms symbolize humility and kindness as well as compassion and fervor. They are prized for the healing qualities both they and the Elder bark offer, which vary from flu remedies to repelling insects.

Since the Elder tree was a death tree, and it was the thirteenth Moon, the number itself became associated with unluckiness.

This time of the year is the darkest of the light. The Sun is dimming and is not yet reborn. Mid-winter Solstice is celebrated around the 21-23 of December as the rebirth of the Sun. Depending upon the culture, the Sun may be a god or a goddess. Call to both, and listen for their answer. In Rome: Apollo or June Lucina; Oma-terasu in Japan; Ra or Horus in Egypt, or Atthar in Arabia.

During the Moon the Yule logs were found and blessed during week-long festivals with the Druids. The burning log was considered to bless the home, but woe unto one which allowed the fire to go out, as this was a sign of ill luck. Part of the Yule log was saved to kindle the fire at the next mid-winter.

Purification of both outer and inner body is the healing power of the Elder. It is said to remedy influenza, and to keep away flies.

APPENDIX D

Recipes

If you'd like to consider making the mead, you will need the following:

CIRCLE MEAD

15 pounds of strained honey
thin peel from 8 lemons
1 packet of yeast
water to make 5 gallons of brew

Pure rainwater is best. Spring water and distilled are also suitable. If you must use tap water from commercial or municipal sources, draw the water up and allow it to sit uncovered for at least twenty-four hours. It is best to avoid it, as the chemicals used in treating the water tend to inhibit the action of the yeast.

A large cooking pot, a long-handled spoon, and a five-gallon glass container will be needed. Once the mead is prepared, a puffy piece of cotton, loose plastic baggie, dark garbage bag, and a warm corner will be needed.

Pour honey into cooking container with heat on medium high. Carefully peel the lemons with a potato peeler or paring knife. Be certain that you obtain only the yellow portion of the rind, as the white part of the peel adds a bitter taste.

If desired, raisins and/or cracked whole nutmeg may be added to this basic recipe for added flavor and enjoyment.

Heat the honey, water, and lemon mixture to a low boil and continue for fifteen minutes. Remove from heat and allow to cool. When the mixture is fully cooled add one packet of ordinary baking yeast (or wine yeast, if desired).

Pour the mixture into a five-gallon GLASS container and place it in a warm place, such as the water-heater closet. Lightly place a puff of cotton in the mouth of the five-gallon jar, cover loosely with a sandwich or similar baggie (unsealed) and then cover entirely with a dark garbage bag or other opaque material.

Allow to sit undisturbed for four to six weeks, checking it periodically during the last two weeks. When the liquid has become comparatively clear and a definite layer of precipitate or sediment has accumulated, then you are ready to siphon the mead into storage containers and enjoy it.

Use a length of clear plastic tubing such as is available in stores which sell and service aquariums. Place the mead container on a table and the bottle to be filled at a lower level. Place one end of the tubing in the mead, being careful NOT to insert it into the sediment at the bottom. With suction, start the mead flowing and fill all necessary containers until approximately one-half to one inch of the clear liquid remains. Do not get the sediment into the siphoned mead. The sediment does not add flavor, but does act as a strong laxative — not a desirable quality for good mead!

Allow the siphoned containers to sit and settle thoroughly. After a time, you may wish to use several layers of soft cheesecloth and carefully pour the siphoned mead into another container, straining it in the process. At that time, rinse the outside of the container, and chill well. My mate prefers to be able to let it sit unused an additional six months, as he feels that the flavor improves with the "aging."

Depending on usage, our coven would generally make at least one batch of mead per year, usually on a Solstice or an Equinox. In any event, enjoy!

HAZEL MOON SALMON BALLS

Place a generous measure of vegetable shortening or oil in a skillet and begin heating it.

Open and drain the liquid from a small can of red salmon. Place the contents in a bowl and break it up with a fork. Add a touch of salt, pepper, and garlic powder, if desired. A small amount of finely chopped onions is optional. I do usually add them, as the white onion is sacred to the Goddess. Stir well. Add one egg and blend all ingredients.

You will need a "filler" of some kind. A small handful of regular soda crackers can be crumbled and blended in, or a handful of corn meal added. Prepared bread crumbs will also serve.

Blend well together, until a light pressure will form a cake or ball that will still cling together. Use a tableware teaspoon to scoop up a heaping spoonful of the salmon mixture. Slide off the spoon into the palm of one hand and begin shaping it into a ball or small cakes. Place them on a saucer or plate and repeat the process. Continue until the oil has heated, and place the balls in the skillet to begin frying. If you place them alternately on either side of the skillet, the cooking temperature will remain more constant. While they begin cooking, complete the formation of balls from the mixture and rinse the mixing bowl.

When the salmon balls are golden-brown on one side, turn them to cook evenly. When the balls are evenly browned on all sides, remove from the skillet and place on absorbent paper or paper towels. Allow to drain thoroughly. Repeat the process until all of the mixture is prepared and cooked.

Cool thoroughly, and place in a covered container. Keep them refrigerated until you are ready for ritual. Place the balls or cakes on a dish or the pantacle and position it at the north of the circle.

That's it. You have the salmon balls or cakes done, the preparation dishes are rinsed or washed, and everything is neat, clean and ready for worship. Incidentally, if the budget is screaming, the small cans of mackerel will substitute for salmon at half the cost! You shouldn't need all of them for ritual unless you are preparing for a very large group. Therefore, the "leftovers" can be eaten for lunch the next day, which makes the can of salmon even more cost-effective.

APPENDIX E

Songs and Chants

We All Come From the Goddess . . .

We all come from the Goddess,
And to her we shall return
Like a drop of rain
Flowing to the Ocean.

We all come from the Horned One,
And to him we shall return
Like a flash of flame
Ascending to the heavens.

Hoof and Horn, Hoof and Horn —
All that dies must be reborn.
Vine and grain, vine and grain —
All that falls shall rise again.

A delightful trio round can be sung, with one part singing the first two stanzas, part two singing the Hoof and Horn segment, and part three singing the following:

Like a drop of rain,
Like a flash of Flame,
Like a voice of Freedom
Coming 'round again . . .

I first heard the Goddess portion of this chant at a gathering in Michigan in 1982. People attending from Canada and from Washington state had developed God chants to balance it. The tri–part round evolved in working of Ev'n Star Coven of Dallas, Texas.
Versions of this song can be found on the album "Catch the Fire" and on "Coming Light — Chants to Honor the Earth Mother" by the Bear tribe.

227

Lady, Weave

Lyrics and music by Llewyn. God verse by Amber Moon Coven.

Lady, Weave your Cir - cle tight. Spin a web of gro-wing light

Earth and Air, and Fire and wa - ter bind us to You.

"Lady, Weave" was shared with me at a Craft gathering in 1980. In 1986, Amber Moon Coven of Oklahoma City shared the God verse they had written to sing with it.

Father, in the coming night . . .
Gather in your Ancient Might.
Sage and Warrior, Horned Hunter.
Guide us to You.

Stir of Breeze

Stir of Breeze, and Blaze of Fire, Flow of wa - ter

Earth De sire, Wax - ing Flow or Fad - ing Light,

Bless the work done in this Rite.

The seven words in the last two measures can be varied as appropriate to the ritual and time of working. Some examples are:

Bless the work we do this night.
Guide the work we do aright.
Bless the work begun tonight.

Weaver, Weaver

Weaver, Weaver, Weave the Web,
Earth, Air, and Fire, Flood Tide and Ebb.

This is a spoken chant, rather than sung. The basic beat is 4/4.

The Goddess is Alive!
The Goddess is Alive! Magic is Afoot!

This chant is a simple, repetitive chant which can be adapted to suit the circumstances or ritual gathering. It is attractive for just joyous celebration or for raising energy.

The Goddess is a Tree.
The Magic is in me!

The Goddess is a Flame;
Brigitte* is Her Name!

(*) or Grainne, or Pele

The Goddess is a Stone.
The Magic is my own!

The Goddess is the Sea!
Her Magic is in Me! (*)

(*) or The Goddess is in Me!

Adapting this spoken chant to relfect the Lord is simply done by using the word "God" rather than "Goddess."

I Bless . . .

I bless Ra, fierce sun burning bright!
I bless Isis, Luna, in the night!
I bless the Air, the Horus Hawk!
I bless the ground upon which I walk!

This is a great attunement chant. Call the blessing for each element. strongly and firmly. When you have achieved contact, then quietly continue the chant until you are restored within. Chant it softly a final time, and end it.

Blood of the Ancients

Shared at a Council of the Magical Arts gathering in Houston, Texas.

Blood of the An cients flows in my veins. The

forms   pass,   But the Cir - cle of Life re-mains.

We are the Old People . . .

We are the Old People; we are the New People;
We are the same People _____ than before.

Verse is repeated, using Wiser, Stronger, Closer, Better, etc., for the variable in the second line.
In Remembrance rites or past life working, one group uses "All we were and more..." as the second half of the last line of the verse. "All we were before..." is effective in doing past life working.

She Changes

She Changes, and everything she changes, Touches.
She Touches, and everything she touches, Changes.

Love Glow, Love Grow!

Shared by Tri–Star Coven, Odessa, Texas.

Wheel of Life

Written for the 1980 NEXUS Celebration .

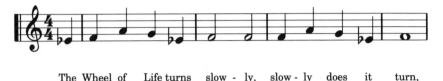

The Wheel of Life turns slow - ly, slow - ly does it turn,

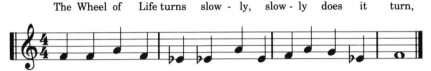

Spring and Sum mer, Har - vest Home, and then the Sun's re - turn.

Witch, I Am!

Lyrics and music by Phoenix Rountree. Arrangement by Garth.

Witch, I am, and Witch, I be: Sis - ter to each

Bud-ding Tree; Air and Fire, Wa - ter, Earth

Wit - ness To my Witch 's Birth!

Cruise to the mountains high
Clouds that gather in the sky.
Kin with Wings and Scales and Fins
Furred Ones roaming woodland glens

Daughter of the Sun and Moon
Harmonizing Nature's tune.
Dancing with the Spirits free.
Witch I am, and Witch I'll be . . .

O Mother Moon

Words from an African tribal song, music by Garth.

O Mother Moon! O   Mother   Moon!   O   Mother   Moon, O   Mother

Moon!   O   Mother   Moon!   O   Mother Moon! O   Mother Moon,   Mother   Moon!

Isis, Astarte

Isis! Astarte!
Diana! Hecate!
Demeter! Kali!
Inanna!

Neptune! Osiris!
Merlin! Manannon!
Helios! Siva!
Horned One!

Pan! Poseidon!
Dionysus! Cernunnos!
Mithras! Loki!
Apollo!

The goddess chant is available on the album, "Catch the Fire"

A paired chant used for drawing down the luminaries was written in 1983 by Tiresias of Circle of the Unicorn. A very strong vortex chant can be created by polarizing a round. Men begin with the God chant, the women with the Goddess portion, switching to the opposite as the next verse in the round, then join together for the paired chant. Try it and feel the energies!

Isis! Osiris!
Hera! Jupiter!
Shakti! Siva!
Ohm . . .

Ecco, Ecco

Ec Co, Ec Co, A ra di a! Ec Co, Ec Co

He - cate and Frey - a! We'll teach your child - ren, year af - ter

Year, To Love with their hearts and live with - out fear.

Our Lady of the Silver Magics,

Lyrics and music by Phoenix Rountree

Teaching Song

Birch moon you may be - gin Strength en my re - solve

Sleep ing moon and know ing time the sa - cred wheel re - volves.

Ro wan wat - tles teach wis dom of the age

stone en - cir - cled o - ra - cle of witch and of the mage.

Stur - dy wa - ter craft born of the cru el ash

Guide my jour ney cross the sea Guard from light ning flash

Al - der bark and branch such a use ful tree

fae - rie tree in ko - re time Heal the doubt in me

Wil - low en - chant - ment moon Bel tain fires a blaze

Po - et and in - ven - tor's tree marked by hawk and haze

Night crow takes its flight in the chas - ti - ty of May.

Haw - thorn fra-grance fills the air. Here the four winds stay.

Great oak mid sum mer tree. Ful - fill - ment of the spring

sa - cred hinge and door am I sol - stice fires I bring.

Dark Lord the Ho - ly oak kills his sac - red twin .

Moon of har - vest star ling flights. The war rior rides with - in.

Wis dom the Ha - zel moon Be wise and de - sist.

Ap - ple wild im - mor - tal tree In - spir - a - tion kissed.

Bac - chus God of wine Bless your sa - cred tree with

au - tumn har vest of the vine We give thanks to thee.

Wild boar and whist - ling swan the hunt - ing horn does sound

With the i - vy and its strength the harv - est bride is bound

Pan pipes of sa - cred reed warn of win - ter's chill

Slen - der shafts do ar - rows make be doth harm or heal

El - der a blood red moon is a tree of wa - ter side

Life in death and death in life in the El - der moon doth hide.

Bibliography

Asimov, Isaac. *The Clock We Live On*. Abelard-Schuman, New York, 1959.

Ber Te. Unpublished Lecture Notes. San Antonio, TX, 1988.

Bleakley, Alan. *Fruits of the Moon Tree*. Gateway Books, London, 1984.

Coe, Michael, with Dean Snow and Elizabeth Benson. *Atlas of Ancient America*. Facts on File, Inc., New York, 1986.

Graves, Robert. *The White Goddess*. Farrar, Straus, and Giroux, New York, 1974.

Gawr, Rhuddlwm. *The Way*. Camelot Press, Atlanta, GA, 1985.

Higgins, Godfrey, Esq., *The Celtic Druids*. The Philosophical Research Society, Los Angeles, CA, 1977.

Llewellyn's 1988 Astrological Calendar. Llewellyn Publications, St. Paul, MN, 1987.

MacCana, Proinsias. *Celtic Mythology*. Peter Redrick Books, New York, 1985.

Markale, Jean. *Women of the Celts*. Harper & Row, New York, 1986.

Parise, Frank, ed., *The Book of Calendars*. Facts on File, Inc., New York, 1974.

Piggot, Stuart, *The Druids*. Thames & Hudson, New York, 1968.

Pike, Donald G., *Anasazi, Ancient People of the Rock.* American West Publishing Co., Palo Alto, CA, 1974.

Redgrove, Peter. *The Black Goddess and the Unseen Real.* Grove Press, New York, 1987.

Ross, Anne. *Druids, Gods & Heroes.* Schoken Books, 1986.

Rutherford, Ward. *Celtic Mythology.* Aquarian Press, Great Britain, 1987.

_____. *The Druids & Their Heritage.* Gordon and Cremonesi Publishers, London, 1978.

_____. *Druids, Magicians of the West.* Aquarian Press, Great Britain, 1978.

Sharkey, John. *Celtic Mysteries.* Thames & Hudson, New York, 1979.

Shearer, Tony. *Beneath the Moon and Under the Sun.* Sun Books, Santa Fe, NM, 1978.

Silverberg, Robert S. *Clocks for the Ages.* Macmillan Publishing Co., New York, 1971.

Thompson, J. Eric, S., *The Rise and Fall of Maya Civilization.* University of Oklahoma Press, Norman, OK.

Umland, Eric & Craig, Walker and Company. *Mystery of the Ancients.* Earth New York, 1974.

Waters, Frank. *Book of the Hopi.* Penguin Books, New York, 1963.

Welch, Kenneth F., David and Charles. *Time Measurement: An Introductory History.* Newton Abbot, Great Britain, 1973.

STAY IN TOUCH

On the following pages you will find listed, with their current prices, some of the books and tapes now available on related subjects. Your book dealer stocks most of these, and will stock new titles in the Llewellyn series as they become available. We urge your patronage.

However, to obtain our full catalog, to keep informed of new titles as they are released and to benefit from informative articles and helpful news, you are invited to write for our bi-monthly news magazine/catalog. A sample copy is free, and it will continue coming to you at no cost as long as you are an active mail customer. Or you may keep it coming for a full year with a donation of just $2.00 in U.S.A. ($7.00 for Canada & Mexico, $20.00 overseas, first class mail). Many bookstores also have *The Llewellyn New Times* available to their customers. Ask for it.

Stay in touch! In *The Llewellyn New Times'* pages you will find news and reviews of new books, tapes and services, announcements of meetiongs and seminars, articles helpful to our readers, news of authors, advertising of products and services, special money-making opportunities, and much more.

The Llewellyn New Times
P.O. Box 64383-Dept. 269, St. Paul, MN 55164-0383, U.S.A.
• • •

TO ORDER BOOKS AND TAPES

If your book dealer does not have the books and tapes described on the following pages readily available, you may order them direct from the publisher by sending full price in U.S. funds, plus $2.00 for postage and handling for the first book, and $.50 for each additional book. There are no postage and handling charges for orders over $50. UPS Delivery: We ship UPS whenever possible. Delivery guaranteed. Provide your street address as UPS does not deliver to P.O. Boxes. UPS to Canada requires a $50 minimum order. Allow 4–6 weeks for delivery. Orders outside the U.S.A. and Canada: Airmail—add retail price of book; add $5 for each non-book item (tapes, etc.); add $1 per item for surface mail.

FOR GROUP STUDY AND PURCHASE

Because there is a great deal of interest in group discussion and study of the subject matter of this book, we feel that we should encourage the adoption and use of this particular book by such groups by offering a special "quantity" price to group leaders or "agents."

Our Special Quantity Price for a minimum order of five copies of *Year of Moons, Season of Trees* is $44.85 cash-with-order. This price includes postage and handling within the United States. Minnesota residents must add 6% sales tax. For additional quantities, please order in multiples of five. For Canadian and foreign orders, add postage and handling charges as above. Credit card (VISA, Master Card, American Express) orders are accepted. Charge card orders only may be phoned free ($15.00 minimum order) within the U.S.A. or Canada by dialing 1-800-THE-MOON. Customer service calls dial 1-612-291-1970. Mail Orders to:

LLEWELLYN PUBLICATIONS
P.O. Box 64383-Dept. 269 / St. Paul, MN 55164-0383, U.S.A.

THE MAGIC IN STONES
by Pattalee Glass-Koentop
The Magic in Stones is a book of possibilities. Pattalee Glass-Koentop lights the way for anyone wishing to create a personal set of runestones. Through understanding the special properties and healing powers of specific stones presented here, you're encouraged to fashion a set of stones symbolically significant to *you* instead of relying on traditional sets with established meanings.

The author's main purpose is to provide you with principles and skills to make well-grounded choices in your life and evolve. Topics covered include:

- Developing psychic awareness
- Learning to "read" your runestones
- Various types of personal readings, from the one-stone"instant" reading to the ninestone reading.
- Casting methods
- New creative systems utilizing heptagrams, hexagrams and the Wheel of life
- Making runestone accessories
- Professionalism, fees and ethics

A novice will be thrilled with the wealth and variety of information presented, eager to delve into more works won this and related subjects. Those familiar with runestones will be spurred on to generate their own special methods.
0-87542-272-1, 264 pgs., 6x9, illus., softcover **$9.95**

BUCKLAND'S COMPLETE BOOK OF WITCHCRAFT
by Raymond Buckland, Ph. D.
Here is the most complete resource to the study and practice of modern, non–denominational Wicca. This is a lavishly illustrated, self–study course for the solitary or group. Included are rituals, exercises for developing psychic talents, and information on all major 'sects' of the Craft, sections on tools, beliefs, dreams, meditations, divination, herbal lore, healing, ritual clothing and much, much more. This book unites theory and practice into a comprehensive course designed to help you develop into a practicing Witch, one of the "Wise Ones." It is written by Dr. Ray Buckland, the very famous and respected authority on witchcraft who first came public with "the Old Religion" in the United States. Large format with workbook–type exercises, profusely illustrated and full of music and chants. Takes you from A to Z in the study of Witchcraft.#
Never before has so much information on "the Craft of the Wise" been collected in one place. Traditionally, there are three degrees of advancement in most Wiccan traditions. When you complete studying this book you will be the equivalent of a "Third Degree Witch." Even those who have practiced Wicca for years find useful information in this book, and many covens are using this for their textbook. If you want to become a Witch, or if you merely want to find out what Witchcraft is really about, you will find no better book than this.
 # 0–87542–050–8, 272 pages, 8–1/2 x 11, illus., softcover **$14.95**

BY STANDING STONE & ELDER TREE
by William Gray
Originally published in 1975 as *The Rollright Ritual*, this book is the re-release of this fascinating work complete with illustrations and a new introduction by the author. The famous stone circle of the "Rollrights" in Oxfordshire, England, is well known to folklorists. Gray, through the use of psychometry,, the retrieved the story of the rocks from the rocks themselves—the story of the culture that placed them and the ritual system used by the ancient stone setters.
This book shows how you can create a Rollright Circle anywhere you wish, even in your own backyard, or within your own mind during meditation. Gray provides specific instructions and a script with an explanation of the language. Even for those not interested in performing the ritual, By Standing Stone & Elder Tree provides an exciting exploration of ancient cultures and of the value that stones hold for the fate of modern civilization.
0–87542–299–3, 208 pages, 5–1/4 x 8, illus., softcover **$9.95**

WHEEL OF THE YEAR: LIVING THE MAGICAL LIFE
by Pauline Campanelli
If you feel elated by the celebrations of the Sabbats and hunger for that feeling during the long weeks between Sabbats, *Wheel of the Year* can help you put the joy and fulfillment of magic into your everyday life. This book shows you how to celebrate the lesser changes in Nature. The wealth of seasonal rituals and charms are all easily performed with materials readily available and are simple and concise enough that the practitioner can easily adapt them to work within the framework of his or her own Pagan tradition.

Learn how to perform fire magic in November, the secret Pagan symbolism of Christmas tree ornaments, the best time to visit a fairy forest or sacred spring and what to do when you get there. Learn the charms and rituals and the making of magical tools that coincide with the nesting season of migratory birds. Whether you are a newcomer to the Craft or found your way back many years ago, *Wheel of the Year* will be an invaluable reference book in your practical magic library. It is filled with magic and ritual for everyday life and will enhance any system of Pagan Ritual.
0–87542–091–5, 159 pgs., 7 x 10, illus., softcover $9.95

CUNNINGHAM'S ENCYCLOPEDIA OF MAGICAL HERBS
by Scott Cunningham

This is an expansion on the material presented in his first Llewellyn book, Mafflcal Herbalism. This is not just another herbal for medicinal uses of herbs–this is the most comprehensive source of herbal data for nia~ca1 uses ever printed! Almost every one of the over 400 herbs are illustrated, making this a great source for herb identification. For each herb you will also find: magical properties, palnetary rulerships, genders, associated deities, folk and Latin names and much more. to make this book even easier to use you will also find a folk name cross reference, and all of the herbs are fully indexed. There is also a large annotated bibliography, and a list of mail order suppliers so you can find the books and herbs you need.
Like all of Scott's books, this one does not require you to use complicated rituals or expensive magical paraphernalia. Instead, it shares with you the intrinsic powers of the herbs. Thus, you will be able to discover which herbs, by their very nature, can be used for luck, love, success, money, divination, astral projection, safety, psychic self–defense and much more. Besides being interesting and educational it is also fun, and fully illustrated with unusual woodcuts from old herbals. This book has rapidly become the classic in its field. It enhances books such as 777 and is a must for all Wiccans.
0–87542–122–9, 352 pgs., 6 x 9, illus., softcover $12.95

WICCA: A GUIDE FOR THE SOLITARY PRACTITIONER
by Scott Cunningham

Wicca is a book of life, and how to live magically, spiritually, and wholly attuned with Nature. It is a book of sense and common sense, not only about Magick, but about religion and one of the most critical issues of today: how to achieve the much needed and wholesome relationship with out Earth. Cunningham presents Wicca as it is today—a gentle, Earth-oriented religion dedicated to the Goddess and God. This book fulfills a need for a practical guide to solitary Wicca—a need which no previous book has fulfilled.Here is a positive, practical introduction to the religion of Wicca, designed so that any interested person can learn to practice the religion alone, anywhere in the world. It presents Wicca honestly and clearly, without the pseudo-history that permeates other books. It shows that Wicca is a vital, satisfying part of twentieth century life.This book presents the theory and practice of Wicca from an individual's perspective. The section on the Standing Stones Book of Shadows contains solitary rituals for the Esbats and Sabbats. This book, based on the author's nearly two decades of Wiccan practice, presents an eclectic picture of various aspects of this religion. Exercises designed to develop magical proficiency, a self-dedication ritual, herb, crystal and rune magic, recipes for Sabbat feasts, are included in this excellent book.
0-87542-118-0, 240 pgs., 6 x 9, illus., softcover $9.95

MAGICAL HERBALISM: The Secret Craft of the Wise
by Scott Cunningham

In Magical Herbalism, certain plants are prized for the special range of energies—the vibrations, or powers—they possess. Magical Herbalism unites the powers of plants and man to produce, and direct, change in accord with human will and desire.This is the Magic of amulets and charms, sachets and herbal pillows, incenses and scented oils, simples and infusions and anointments. It's Magic as old as our knowledge of plants, an art that anyone can learn and practice, and once again enjoy as we look to the Earth to rediscover our roots and make inner connections with the world of Nature.This is Magic that is beautiful and natural—a Craft of Hand and Mind merged with the Power and Glory of Nature: a special kind that does not use the medicinal powers of herbs, but rather the subtle vibrations and scents that touch the psychic centers and stir the astral field in which we live to work at the causal level behind the material world.This is the Magic of Enchantment . . . of word and gesture to shape the images of mind and channel the energies of the herbs. It is a Magic for *everyone*—for the herbs are easily and readily obtained, the tools are familiar or easily made, and the technology that of home and garden. This book includes step-by-step guidance to the preparation of herbs and to their compounding in incense and oils, sachets and amulets, simples and infusions, with simple rituals and spells for every purpose.
0-87542-120-2, 256 pgs., 5 1/4 x 8, illus., softcover $7.95

THE MAGICAL HOUSEHOLD
by Scott Cunningham and David Harrington

Whether your home is a small apartment or a palatial mansion, you want it to be something special. Now it can be with TheMafflcalHousehold. Learn how to make your home more thanjusta place to live. Turn it into a place of security, life, fun and magic. Here you will not find the complex magic of the ceremonial magician. Rather, you will learn simple, quick and effective magical spells 'that use nothing more than common items in your house: furniture, windows, doors, carpet, pets, etc. You will learn to take advantage of the intrinsic power and energy that is already in your home, waiting to be tapped. You will learn to make magic a part of your life. The result is a home that is safeguarded from harm and a place which will bring you happiness, health and more.
ISBN: 0–87542–124–5, illus., softcover $8.95

IN THE SHADOW OF THE SHAMAN
by Amber Wolfe

Presented in what the author calls a "cookbook shamanism" style, this book shares recipes, ingredients, and methods of preparation for experiencing some very ancient wisdoms—wisdoms of Native American and Wiccan traditions, as well as contributions from other philosophies of Nature, as they are used in the shamanic way. Wolfe encourages us to feel confident and free to use her methods to cook up something new, completely on our own. This blending of ancient formulas and personal methods represents what Ms. Wolfe calls *Aquarian Shamanism*.

In the Shadow of the Shaman is designed to communicate in the most practical, direct ways possible, so that the wisdom and the energy may be shared for the benefits of all. Whatever your system or tradition, you will find this to be a valuable book, a resource, a friend, a gentle guide and support on your journey. Dancing in the shadow of the shaman, you will find new dimensions of Spirit.
0-87542-888-6, 384 pgs., 6 x 9, illus., softcover $12.95

CELTIC MAGIC
BY D. .J. Conway

Many people, not all of Irish descent, have a great interest in the ancient Celts and the Celtic pantheon, and *Celtic Magic* is the map they need for exploring this ancient and fascinating magical culture.*Celtic Magic* is for the reader who is either a beginner or intermediate in the field of magic, providing an extensive "how-to" of practical spell-working. There are many books on the market dealing with the Celts and their beliefs, but none guide the reader to a practical application of magical knowledge for use in everyday life. There is also an in-depth discussion of Celtic deities and the Celtic way of life and worship, so that an intermediate practitioner can expand upon the spellwork to build a series of magical rituals.Presented in an easy-to-understand format. *Celtic Magic* is for anyone searching for new spells that can be worked immediately, without elaborate or rare materials, and with minimal time and preparation.

0-87542-136-9, 240 pgs., mass market, illus. **$3.95**

EARTH POWER:
TECHNIQUES OF NATURAL MAGIC
by Scott Cunningham

Magick is the art of working with the forces of Nature to bring about necessary, and desired, changes. The forces of Nature—expressed through Earth, Air, Fire and Water—are our "spiritual ancestors" who paved the way for our emergence from the pre-historic seas of creation. Attuning to, and working with these energies in magick not only lends you the power to affect changes in your life, it also allows you to sense your own place in the larger scheme of Nature. Using the "Old Ways" enables you to live a better life, and to deepen your understanding of the world about you. The tools and powers of magick are around you, waiting to be grasped and utilized. This book gives you the means to put Magick into your life, shows you how to make and use the tools, and gives you spells for every purpose.

0-87542-121-0, 176 pgs., 51/4 x 8, illus., softcover **$8.95**

MAGICAL RITES FROM THE CRYSTAL WELL
by Ed Fitch

In nature, and in the earth, we look and find beauty. Within ourselves we find a well from which we may draw truth and knowledge. And when we draw from this well, we rediscover that we are all children of the Earth.The simple rites in this book are presented to you as a means of finding your own way back to nature; for discovering and experiencing the beauty and the magic of unity with the source. These are the celebrations of the seasons; at the same time they are rites by which we attune ourselves to the flow of the force—the energy of life. These are rites of passage by which we celebrate the major transitions we all experience in life.Here are the Old Ways, but they are also the Ways for Today.

0-87542-230-6, 147 pgs., 7 x 10, illus., softcover **$9.95**

THE LLEWELLYN ANNUALS

Llewellyn's MOON SIGN BOOK: Approximately 400 pages of valuable information on gardening, fishing, weather, stock market forecasts, personal horoscopes, good planting dates, and general instructions for finding the best date to do just about anything! Article by prominent forecasters and writers in the fields of gardening, astrology, politics, economics and cycles. This special almanac, different from any other, has been published annually since 1906. It's fun, informative and has been a great help to millions in their daily planning.

State year $4.95

Llewellyn's SUN SIGN BOOK: Your personal horoscope for the entire year! All 12 signs are included in one handy book. Also included are forecasts, special feature articles, and an action guide for each sign. Monthly horoscopes are written by Gloria Star, author of *Optimum Child*, for your personal Sun Sign and there are articles on a variety of subjects written by well-known astrologers from around the country. Much more than just a horoscope guide! Entertaining and fun the year around.

State year $4.95

Llewellyn's DAILY PLANETARY GUIDE and ASTROLOGER'S DATEBOOK: Includes all of the major daily aspects plus their exact times in Eastern and Pacific time zones, lunar phases, signs and voids plus their times, planetary motion, a monthly ephemeris, sunrise and sunset tables, special articles on the planets, signs, aspects, a business guide, planetary hours, rulerships, and much more. Large 5 1/4 x 8 format for more writing space, spiral bound to lay flat, address and phone listings, time zone conversion chart and blank horoscope chart.

State year $6.95

Llewellyn's ASTROLOGICAL CALENDAR: Large wall calendar of 52 pages. Beautiful full color cover and color inside. Includes special feature articles by famous astrologers, introductory information on astrology. Lunar Gardening Guide, celestial phenomena, a blank horoscope chart for your own chart data, and monthly date pages which include aspects, lunar information, planetary motion, ephemeris, personal forecasts, lucky dates, planting and fishing dates, and more. 10 x 13 size. Set in Central time, with conversion table for other time zones worldwide.

State year $9.95

Llewellyn's MAGICKAL ALMANAC
Edited by Ray Buckland

The Magickal Almanac allows the reader a peek behind a veil of secrecy into Egyptian, Shamanic, Wiccan and other traditions. Almanac pages for each month provide sunrise and sunset, phases and signs of the Moon, and festival dates, as well as the tarot card, herb, incense, color, and name of power (god/goddess/entity) associated with the particular day.

Each month, following the almanac pages, are articles addressing one form of Magick, with rituals the reader can easily follow. An indispensible guide for all interested in the Magickal arts, *The Magickal Almanac* features writing by some of the most prominent authors in the field.

State year $9.95

THE GODDESS BOOK OF DAYS
by Diane Stein

Diane Stein has created this wonderful guide to the Goddesses and festivals for every day of the year! This beautifully illustrated perpetual datebook will give you a listing for every day of the special Goddesses associated with that date along with plenty of room for writing in your appointments. It is a hardbound book for longevity, and has over 100 illustrations of Goddesses from around the world and from every culture. This is sure to have a special place on your desk. None other like it!

0–87542–758–8, 300 pgs., hardbound, illus.   **$12.95**